I0741423

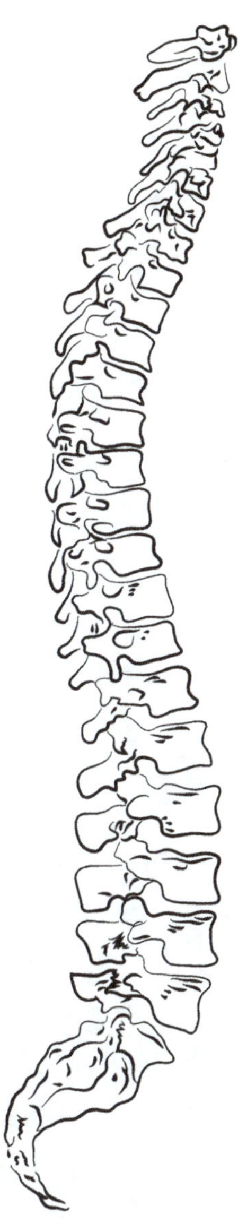

THIRTY THREE

An[niversary] Anthology

At once it struck me what quality went to form a Man of Achievement, especially in Literature, and which Shakespeare possessed so enormously—I mean Negative Capability, that is, when a man is capable of being in uncertainties, mysteries, doubts, without any irritable reaching after fact and reason.

—John Keats

Negative Capability
PRESS
MOBILE, ALABAMA

Publisher/Editor-in-Chief

Sue Brannan Walker

Editors

Bailey Hammond
Karie Fugett
Rachel McMullen

Art Director/Cover Designer

Megan Cary

Negative Capability Press was founded in Mobile, Alabama, and
has been publishing award winning books since 1981. Negative
Capability Press is a Member of APSS: Association of Publishers for
Special Sales (formerly SPAN). Wholesale and distribution is available
through Small Press Distribution (SPD). For a list of other titles
published go to negativecapabilitypress.org.

Negative Capability Press
62 Ridgelawn Drive East
Mobile, Alabama 36608

www.negativecapabilitypress.org
facebook.com/negativecapabilitypress
marketing@negativecapabilitypress.org

International Standard Serial Number (ISSN) 0227-5166
ISBN 978-0-942544-26-8

THIRTY THREE

the number of years that Negative Capability Press has
been publishing

the number of vertebrae in the human spine

the atomic number of arsenic

the temperature that water boils

the Triangulum galaxy

the number of miracles that Jesus performed

the smallest sum of two positive numbers, each of which raised
to the fifth power: $1^5 + 2^5 = 33$.

the largest positive integer that cannot be expressed as a sum of
different triangular numbers. It is also the smallest odd repdigit
that is not a prime number.

the eighth distinct semiprime comprising the prime factors (3
• 11). Its aliquot sum is 15; itself a discrete semiprime (3 • 5) in
the following Aliquot sequence 33,15,9,4,3,1,0. (Note 33 is the
8th composite number to descend into the prime number 3, the
others outside of this sequence being 30,26,16,12) Since 33 is a
semiprime with both its prime factors being Gaussian primes, 33
is a Blum integer.

Negative Capability's *Thirty Three* Anthology is organic,
scientific, innovative, astonishing, a little strange—an odd
number, indeed, and is certainly capable of being in uncertainty.

CONTENTS

TRANSLATION FROM THE FRENCH

TRANSLATION FROM THE SPANISH

REACHING AFTER FACT

Dick Allen

WHEN THE FIRST QUAIL CALLS
For Pete Seegar

Whether at night or morning, when you hear that
first quail call, those three bubbling amphibrachs,
the way they sound like someone lifting water from a well,
the pulley whining and pausing as it guides the rope,
something also pauses in you, something with nothing
to do with cell phones, or computers, or microwaves,
but goes back to evenings when stars spread across the sky
like punch-holes in an old piano roll, or mornings
rising damply out of the mist floating on southern rivers,
and you stand, hands clenched at your sides,
listening, trying to hold onto it: *chuk-wee-stan,*
chuk-wee-stan, chuck-wee-stan
as if it's Cherokee, or Seminole, or Apache,
sounds so woven into American life
we barely give them thought: *Schenectady,*
Yoknapatawpha, Missouri. So when that first quail calls,
all still seems possible. You can believe
in a time before GPS, iTunes, the instant
broken into micro-instants, the Rock Island Line,
all the synthetics in which we clothe ourselves—
the time of the Drinking Gourd,
"Jimmy crack corn and I don't care,"
when quail ran in the forests, joyousness about them,
with their coveys and plumes,
and you looked into shadows, expecting shadows
to lighten and dissolve into fields and meadows and low hills,
into clear paths through the brush,
and the shadows looked at you back,
as everything returns your gaze if you look deeply enough,
to say all promises shall be kept,
chuk-wee-stan, chuk-wee-stan, chuck-wee-stan,
this night or morning, when the first quail calls.

Maureen Alsop

PRELIMINARY

The antique hills half far, my fingers salted, stone rosettes cling to my anklet. Palms wave seaward.

Suppose the silt of the river traveled the valley: the full lake renounced the heat: birch in the heartland of surrounds: and we were not enough to be held.

Shut one admission, against forest, sorrel. Empty handed in the doorway. Geraniums dried between every other growing. All through the battle light remained unnatural. Without stillness you surrendered as if entering into a new descent. Seizure of snow. Quiet pages, you turned the lane loose with white.

Rae Armantrout

THE SCORE

1

One poet
slips out of

what each sentence
begins to say—

a magician
freeing himself

from the underwater
cage.

2

"They tell me I got this
 Alzheimer's. I don't

know," he says
to the moderator,

as if doubt
were a way

to catch
one's fall

3

Folds
in the clear

curtains, columns
at dusk

scored by slant
ripples,

 marked by stacked
apexes,

making some points

David B. Axelrod

SEEING THINGS AS THEY ARE

First, it was my eyes, framed
in a rear-view mirror, staring
at me—so much older than
the driver rushing toward some
self-appointed task. There are
old souls—children who know
more than they should. I saw
the backhand of abuse, the fist
of prejudice long before I aged.
But now I see my hands, holding
every ailment—from liver spots
to large, stiff knuckles and thin,
stretched skin over piano-wire
tendons. I object to poems about
poetry—the pretention of asking,
"What hand holds this pen?"
Surely, there are better things
than idle self-absorption. But,
these hands have seized
the moment. Don't blame me
if I am forced to cover my eyes.

Walter Bargen

COLLARED

He lost his dog and still he grips the collar in his hand trying not to let go. Arm out-stretched, his body turned sideways, he's yanked along by what isn't there. He refuses not to see four long legs, floppy ears the length of shoe tongues, Groucho Marx eyebrows, a two-tone tail curved up except when thunder beats at the windows. He's doggedly tried not to lay blame but responsibility lies curled up on the couch and cowering in a corner.

In the yard, he secures the collar around an oak tree. He offers it an old soup bone. He listens to the tree bark. It howls its leaves into the sky. A hind leg of wind scratches vigorously. He walks in circles around the tree. This is how the road goes on forever or the path until the webbing frays and the lead snaps. Then the tree runs off and his business is no longer circumference. He's left with the straight and narrow arrow of grief.

Soon he's collared the table. Tries to walk a chair but it keeps falling on the first step down the stairs. The lamp chases the tail of its own light knocking papers from the desk onto the floor. At the last, he waits by the door to be let out, pacing back and forth, the spiked collar around his neck, the leash in his hands, determined this time to not let himself run away to the dogs again.

Fred Bassett

ON PALATINE HILL

The rueful quietness
of the mystic ruins
soothes his senses,
drummed numb by the noise
of jabber-day Rome.
Then the disquietude,
the ebbing twilight.
Darkness will catch him
and push him back
into the milling throngs
of the Eternal City.

Behold! A woman
descending the path,
her scarlet dress
fluid as her raven hair.
He steps aside.
She stops, sweet of scent.
He knows the smile,
but those dark eyes
turn him up the hill
to ponder the last
ruin of the day.

Jack B. Bedell

First Kiss

I cannot keep my daughter's mind
off baby frogs. My father caught one
for her the other day and put it
in the hollow of her palm. She fell
for its smooth green skin and shiny eyes,
loved how it held her fingertips
in its tiny hands. Now she's a huntress.

As soon as the coffee pot goes off
in the morning, she's dressed
and staring out the back-door glass,
waits on point until I release the bolt,
setting her to motion. There's no
distracting her with linguistics, the difference
between *crapaud* and *ouaouaron*. She wants

to turn over every pot, pull back
the cover on the barbecue pit,
check each slat in the storm shutters.
She knows no crack is too small
for these frogs. They can flatten themselves
and get under anything. They fold their bones
and wait for her, each one a prince.

Charles Bernstein

Passing

(after Tin Moe and ko ko thett)

Stogie smoked
Sun set
Take me home

Joyce Brinkman

Overcoming

We meet in clouds, our separate cells unite.
Small specks from each ascend the air like kites.
    Like birds that seek a cliff on which to nest,
    they rise beyond earth's conflicts finding rest
in joining water, dust and smoke in flight.

With past earthly variations seeming trite,
now scattered colors fuse and blend to white.
    Floating North toward South, or East to West,
        we meet in clouds.

They glisten in gold rays of healing light.
They dance about the sky to our delight.
    Could we find beauty long before this quest?
    Could wars and strife, injustice be addressed?
When cells we wear decline to cling skintight,
        we meet in clouds

John J. Brugaletta

AN ANCIENT LETTER ENGLISHED

Beloved Festus, I am pleased to say
your latest missive has arrived, and I
have smiled for several hours as a result.
You offer us apologies for what
you shyly term your less-than-noble birth.
No such apologies are needed, friend,
for every family, at some remove,
had slaves and brigands to infect its beds.

Now on to answering your inquiries
on ways to cloak one's body's ruder acts.
And first, the dreaded fecatorium:
The scent one leaves behind is best dealt with
by lighting in the room a candle's wick.
Wave this about so that the flame will catch
and burn away the inconvenient cloud.
You'll hear the light report, a distant "whoof,"
together with a moment's brightening.
If this should fail to time with laughter's noise,
the guests are sure to think it flatulence.
But if, when you rejoin the group, they laugh
and look on you, just point at one of them
and laugh the louder. This will make them think
you know a thing they did not comprehend,
confounding all their ridicule of you.

And then to picking of your nose. Do not.
I lay this down as law, dear Festus. No!
In company, the servants surely have
a store of little cloths to blow your nose.
On taking one of these, turn outward from
your nearer friends and softly blow away.
(The same device will serve for sudden coughs.)
Take care, however, when this act is done
you do not peer into the napkin's fold
as if to search for pearls your brain expelled.
This would undo all cautions heretofore.

You also ask about your itching ear.
I've seen you do it. In your finger goes,
which waggles you so energetically
your head goes bobbing and your eyes protrude.
I fear long habit will prevent a change
in how you scratch your ear. All I can do
is to advise it done in private rooms.
And this will serve as well for other spots
that itch and are best scratched in privacy.
Part not your toga where fine ladies watch,
no matter how a flea torments your groin.

Think not, my Festus, that these rules are all
a gentleman must heed to be soigné.
But these will start you on the lengthy climb
to social altitude and thinner air.
Forget not bathing, pare your fingernails,
and gargle with your wife's perfume to mask
the potent garlic that you love to chew.

Joe Cavanaugh

TRAPPED IN A NUMBERS GAME

I'm pinned down
My time is up
If I can't remember the number
I will lose everything

seconds before the
waterboarding begins
I remember it might be

the exact date and time of my first kiss
Or maybe the cubic inches of engine displacement in my 1961 Chevy
Could it be the number of the house where we stole the weathervane
From the barn late that night

The red light blinks
I enter the personal identification number
The steel door swings open
I hear a computerized voice
I've got mail

John Chambers

ALONE

Midnight.
Distant trains wail.
Stairs creak.
Floors groan.
A sudden rush of wind
moves the porch shades.

Silence hovers
over the house.
Only solitude walks
about—one heavy
step nearer.

Kelly Cherry

OF LOVE AND TIME

Time felt expands and shrinks according to
the number of details that we observe.
The less familiar an experience,
the more details we notice, lengthening
the time it takes; and the more ordinary,
the fewer details adhere. And yet your face,
better known to me than is my name,
and creased and folded like a well-used map,
is a place in which I'd live a million years
if I could, every year a century,

every century a millennium

and all that lengthy while I'll register
the play of light upon your light green eyes,
silver stubble and mobile mouth, the way
you clear your throat to say a thing clever
or punning. Such minute observations
to me are Shakespeherian dramaturgy
and bespeak a narrative of close detail
that makes each single moment as riveting
as insight and as lingering as a poem
about the inexhaustible theme of love.

Peter Cooley

SUMMERTIME

First day of summer when you were a child,
the morning school was over until fall.
Remember how you slept a little late, then woke
to feel the day was open like the sky,
the windows watching you, your room their blue?
You'd never have to go to school again.

Fifty, sixty years later I've gone back
to be that child again: sun on my face
waking in June, waking without a rush
to go, to be, to do, to carry on
some fragment of my life from yesterday.

This picture holds time-still and dying-still.
You can be both the mother and the girl
and the-ducks-stared-at and the wide water,
everything held in suspension of the past.
You can be watched and watcher, stilled and still.

In response to:
Summertime, Mary Cassatt, 1894
Oil on canvas
The Armand Hammer Foundation, Los Angeles, California

Chris Crittenden

A LACK

mirrors bathed the streets
in cloggy cataract grey.
snowflakes, like confused pilgrims,
skittered on crystal esplanades,
cursed by weightless moebius strips
and golgothas.

not even molecules could hide,
exposed in woebegone slices
of a diffused and senile sun.
sparkles perched in canvases of ice,
mysterious as alien birds,
spread-eagled and fluted.

hope belonged
to a blizzard's prestissimo;
to an anti-sound of music
only disappearance could savor.
snowbanks, once hillocks of the pure,
had matted into ziggurats
of motor oil and suds.

we were a city of exiles
couched in prisons of plaster,
as unwelcome and awkward
as a Ragnarok of giants,
wearing an alien softness
of impossible fire.

we needed the icicles in windy jaws
to bookmark our memories;
to transform into brave flags
that heralded a lost outpost
of resolute tradition.

we begged the night
to offer us a jigger of Venus;
to cherish one crisp drop of her
under the fanged and titanic sorcery
of bedeviled stars.

Emmanuel Damon

PRÉDATION

À pas comptés   Prédation
Et remords dans la neige nouvelle va le loup
Il quitte le couvert et la volaille s'agite
Le ciel est d'argent clair le sang
Dans les gorges palpite au printemps revenu
Sous le givre léger la mer est muette les armes
À l'affût sommeillent
La faim cette clarté
C'est entendre et prévoir
Le loup avance sans phrases gorge nue sa syntaxe
Appartient au couvert sous les balles
Ses flancs sont de bois tendre sur le drap tendu de la neige

Translated by Isabele Whitman

With measured tread walking   Depredation
And remorse in the new snow a wolf goes
Out of the shelter and chicken bustle around
The sky is clear silver   Blood
In the throats pound as spring is back
In the light rime the sea is silent   Weapons
In wait sleep
Hunger this light hears and foresees
The wolf comes with no words bare throat
His syntax belongs to shelter under the bullets
His flanks are gentle wood on the laid sheet of the snow

Kristina Darling

from THE SUN & THE MOON

(IX)

From the start, I knew that our marriage was one of practicality. You always said beauty can be a form of service. So every night, the ghosts would watch me straighten my dress, fasten my veil & button my long silk gloves. For awhile, it kept them from looting the armoire, or worse, starting those small fires in the vestibule. I did what I could to keep the house from burning. Soon they see me all shimmering in white & can barely speak. You just stand there & stare, your suit covered in ash, the altar catching fire behind you.

(X)

You were never quite sure about my dress, the way its cold silk trailed through the city below. Still I'd fasten the veil, straighten my sleeves & button those long white gloves. I waited & waited, but you never seemed to make up your mind. The fire grew smaller & the room darker. My dress was smudged with soot. Before long I'd see a flash of light in the doorway, the groom everyone else was afraid of. That's what I loved about you. Somehow you just stand there, a handkerchief folded in your front pocket, the room burning all around you.

(XI)

One night, after you'd finished tending the fire, you told me the truth about the ghosts. They had been the smallest stars in a grand constellation, which lit the streets in the city below. Then piece by piece, the sky darkened. The stars held their breath & before long they felt the weight of their clothes shifting. Their dresses crackled with frost. That was when they began walking from house to house, fumbling with the silver locks on every door. You recognized them only by the cold light shining from each of their perfectly shaped mouths.

John Davis Jr.

Dock Thieving

We went to find our echoes that August.
All summer, they'd summoned us across Lake Arrow,
and that day, we took Doc Muncy's dock to answer.

Uprooting pipes staking it to shore, Hank
assured me we'd be fine—*Borrowing is only half-
stealing.* He pushed us off with a dead limb of hickory.

When retiree fishermen in their jonboat
questioned our raft, Hank was cordial, jovial:
We're earning our merit badges for jerry-rigging.

On the far edge, hard structures talked back to us:
Bigger houses than ours leered unfamiliar
and dark as their ancestral plots underneath.

We returned, fixed the dock back to the sand where
we'd freed it, and uttered nothing on the walk
west to home. Sound was so many empty waves.

Nandini Dhar

INHERITANCE

Inside our mother's womb, frangipanis bloom in profusion. We peep through her belly button: the staircase, the mango tree in the corner of the courtyard, the gourd vine. Four in the morning, and our mother is brewing tea. The familiar refrain of Rabindranath in her voice and the sound of her lips slurping. This quiet hour when she gathers hibiscus pollen in her open palms. Who doesn't know that the sun is nothing but an over-baked bread who cannot live without heralding the obligatory: the to-do-lists, what is to be done. I dream of another century—the nineteenth. And, my sister carves a canoe. For herself and our stillborn brothers. We both know during those hours of barging out, my sister had tried to strangle me. My princess farce—a little girl in magenta satin riding a rocking horse diagonally across the tea plantations of our mother's childhood dreams. I bury my unease into the crevices of the tunes our mother hums—they grow into something else: jealousy. Am I being left out from my sister's plans? In the kitchen, girls are dusting their fake cartileges. Our cousins. My mother settles her eyes on the chameleon on the moss-green wall, watches it suck blood out of her swollen belly. My sister keeps denying. Claims, it was nothing: just the whir of our aunt catching rainbows in the detergent bubbles while handwashing the men's underwears. Just our great-grandmother charming up the stitches in her old tapestries, wounding them around my neck. *Hold still, stand still*—my sister commands. That's the sound of our great-grandmother braiding together her love and rage into a prayer mat. You cannot buy it anywhere. *Hold still and let her cut off your oxygen.*

Melissa Dickson

APPLES AND EDAM

For Britta and Mette

Mary said you couldn't bring them back,
it didn't work that way. She was a new friend,
older and not inclined to sentiment—about food

or people. But there I was, a guest in her kitchen,
the beaches of St. George beyond the shutters,
a Fuji apple split open at its seeded heart,

a block of Edam cheese, room temperature,
and soft enough to tear apart with my fingertips.
That's what I ate those three days, apples and Edam,

an occasional slice of heavy-grain German bread.
Because I was off the coast of Florida in a house
of busy women. Fish camps and sun bathers dimpling

the shore. Because in that busy house I was alone,
or lonely, or just sentimental. Because what I wanted
was to take again our grand journey, twenty years distant.

Britta on the train to Prague. Mette on the ferry from Aarhus.
My dumb-self kneeling at Karen Blixen's grave
as though I had known and loved her. In the knapsack—

butter and cheese sandwiches, three apples.
In the days to come, we girls will take trains
through Medieval towns and industrial villages

and find not one green thing on the restaurant menus:
sausages and boiled dough, beer, stewed meat, pickled cabbage.
There will be bell towers, and churches, and tourists,

orchestras composed of dental assistants and street sweepers.
There will be a fruit vendor selling navel oranges.
And the one I buy for us to share will taste as sweet

as the one I cut open with a stranger's pocketknife
on an Amtrak train from Boston, alone, learning what it was
I wanted from the world in the days before I knew.

Chantel Enright

CON EL AMOR

Con el amor del trazo en furia
se abre la sombra
tu pluma
hacia ti prìncipe de nuestra ausencia
tu pincel propone su imagen
se moldea y pasea fábulas inexistentes

Translated by Irene Marks

By love traced in fury
shadow is opened
your pen
towards you prince of our absence
your brush proposes its image
is shaped and moves nonexistent fables

Beth Ann Fennelley

Do the Dead Know What Time it Is?

Remember, now, those silent dawns in the suburbs
gazing out at the shroud of appalling snow
and noticing the prints, the many crisp punctures:
animals had circled the house during the night
sewing their legs, for a moment, through the white cloak
strange, you'd never guessed
they existed, much less visited

Jennifer Grant

THE SHAME OF RED LIPSTICK

Do college co-eds still call it 'The Walk of Shame'—a nickname given the journey from a lover's bed to the getaway car parked out front? I've also known it as the morning-after march, one that percolates penance for a night of reckless wickedness. With bed-head hair, no change of clothes (not even a toothbrush), each step to escape the lust nest undiscovered proving trickier than the last. As I watch it unfold in my rearview mirror, a wretched grin kisses my lips. It's a rerun of a show from over a decade ago during my earlier debauched existence.

Before I convinced him to wed, I often fled my beloved's sloshing waterbed and its tawdry existence. As the sun blushed the sky (like today), I'd slink back to my southern sorority house in shame. I departed early enough (or at least tried) to avoid frat brothers' jeers and the silent judgment that seeped from the House Mother's pursed lips.

Today, it's a new nubile woman who stands tall and proud, braiding her brown hair down her back and zipping her jacket tight up her front. She leans over and fixes her fuzzy, shin high boots, making this chilly, shameful moment almost elastic. She breathes in the freshness and novelty of early morning light, unaware of her exact wickedness.

I suffer a rush of guilt, a stalker on surveillance of a modern day Jezebel who's one with her wickedness. I'm analyzing her like an endangered creature exposed in a wild existence. I stay focused as the graceful gazelle takes her time trotting her long, lanky legs from the neon lit Motel 6 across the street (my own, personal iconoclast)! An orange Volkswagen bug awaits her, along with her shame. I appreciate her façade of strength and poise on desire's battlefront. It makes the next moment so sweet I can nearly taste Eve's apple on my lips.

When the gazelle girl realizes her secret has been exposed, a bewildered O forms on her lips. Now the price will be paid for her wickedness. But her reaction is an affront. Doesn't she care that someone now knows of her existence? Doesn't she feel shame? I observe her reading what I scrawled in streetwalker red lipstick that department store cosmetic clerk promised would last:

'WHORE—not the first, but the last.'

I lick my dry, cracked lips. I am unashamed. This is her penalty for unwedded wickedness. But instead of panicking, she pulls a pair of pink underwear from her purse and wipes away the words, their existence. She bobs her head around, searching for the author, as if one would be found in the forefront. To avoid discovery, I shift my car into reverse, unprepared to confront. My mission completed at last. I have revealed my existence. I glance at the back seat where my babies sleep, each with sealed lips. I ease my tan minivan out of its space and head to Mama's house where I'll relay the entire affair and my husband's continued wickedness. It is all such a God damned shame.

When the tears start, I stop my vehicle shorefront, where I shakily pull out my last tube of crimson to fix my lips. I will no longer cry, nor be trapped in my spouse's web of wickedness. I lock the windows and the doors and push the pedal to the floor, ready to expunge my little family's existence, rather than drown in a sea of small town shame.

Robert Gray

OBJECTIVE EXPERIENCE

life is reading an effort
to find music in the prosaic

the alliteration of the landscape
the enjambments of experience
and daily interaction

the metonymic semiotics
of perception i like to dwell

where image confronts thought
where consciousness
encounters the real as language

as poetry we each learn
different lessons in our reading

of reality i like to inhabit the meta-
elements of the construct
where beauty is in the finding

of the façade in the act
of translating sense

into the language of thought
of converting the world into language
into the currency of consciousness

which not only mediates the objective
it is the objective

poets long ago wrote of how
we half-create the scenes we
perceive of how we all may look

upon a tree of how we never seem
to see the exact same tree

WANDERLUST AWAY

Bronwyn Sellers hated her name. She awoke each morning to the sound of AntiBelle calling her to roll out of bed and get dressed for school. AntiBelle's whiskey and smoke voice made her name sound like two frogs mating.

"Bron-wyn! Bro-o-o-n-wyn!"

She hated her name, and she hated high school, and she hated Meridian, Mississippi, the town that would neither grow nor die. It clung to the edge of life like Gilda McAdams, Suttie McAdams' wheezing, camphor-smelling grandmother. Some afternoons, when Bronwyn was in the McAdams' house playing computer games or listening to music with Suttie, they could hear Granny McAdams' horrid gasping in the sick room next door. They would catch themselves, eyes wide and breath held, listening for her to stop. It was awful, and far too funny. They would slap each other's arms and laugh so hard they had to smother the sound with pillows.

And that was about the most exciting thing happening in Meridian.

Bronwyn pulled on her school polo shirt and navy skirt, passed a hairbrush through her pale blond curls, and hurried downstairs to the kitchen where AntiBelle had scrambled eggs, biscuits, homemade mayhaw jelly, and grits steaming on a plate. All she had to do was salt the food and shovel it into her mouth.

"Your mama would smack you upside the head for eating like an animal." AntiBelle leaned toward her from the other side of the counter. She had on false eyelashes at least three-quarters of an inch long and she'd drawn a fake mole on the right side of her mouth. At least Bronwyn thought it was fake. She didn't recall ever seeing it before, and AntiBelle was quite capable of coming to the house in a disguise. Bronywn examined the black mark for a hair. A hair would prove it to be real.

"And quit staring. It's rude. Your mama is flipping cartwheels in her grave at the way you're growing up. Not one shred of manners or social graces. Heaven help you if you ever decide to leave Meridian. If the gypsies still traveled through here they'd pick you up and put you in a tent show as 'the human garbage disposal.'"

"Gypsies are too smart to come to Meridian. They'd die of boredom the minute they arrived."

"Shows what you know, little Missy. They used to come through here all the time. One time they stole your mama and it took Miss Margaret five days to track them down and get Ella Rae back. Everyone in town was terrified something bad had happened to El, but she was perfectly fine. I wasn't worried. She was just trying to find—" AntiBelle stopped talking. "She wanted adventure."

Bronwyn straightened her posture and slowed the rate of the fork to her lips. This was a new story. No one talked to her about her mother, except AntiBelle, and that wasn't very often. "How old was Mama when they took her?"

"Oh, about your age."

Bronwyn was shocked. She'd assumed her mother was a child. Gypsies stole children. "Did she leave with them? Voluntarily?"

AntiBelle blinked the heavy eyelashes. "That's not the way I heard the story. She was taken." She shrugged. "But I never asked your mama. El was fragile, but she could be tough, too. Like you. As far as I know she never talked about it. Not a word about the five days she was gone. Think about that. To never tell a soul about such an adventure. But it changed her. I don't think her mother ever forgave her."

"Do the gypsies still come through town?"

"All the time. Their king and queen are buried in Rose Hill Cemetery."

Bronwyn heard the car horn. Suttie's mother always blew the horn, a fact that rankled AntiBelle.

"That Blanche McAdams knows it's rude to blow a horn. Suttie should get out of the car and knock at the door like civilized people. No manners. It's a virus spreading through all you young people. After your mama…well, I took on the job of raising you up proper and I have failed."

Bronwyn enjoyed AntiBelle's melodrama. "I have manners. I know how to behave. And you're a fine one to talk."

"What is it you think you know, little Missy?" She tapped the counter with her manicured red nails. "Put it out right here on this red granite that your mama loved. Spill it before you run off to school."

Bronwyn fought down her laughter. "I don't even know your real name. All I know is AntiBelle because you refused to answer to your given name and told your mama you'd *never* be a Meridian socialite.

You burned your wedding gown and wore a feed sack to the altar, and cancelled the wedding with half of Meridian already seated in the First Methodist Church. You scandalized the entire congregation and most of the county."

Antibelle's clear laughter rang out in the kitchen. "Lord, girl, where do you get your stories?"

Bronwyn wasn't surprised. When cornered, AntiBelle could lie like a rug. It was one of her favorite things about her. "People talk. In fact, that's all they do in Meridian. Jabber, jabber, gossip, jabber. And they talk about you plenty."

"I 'spect they do. And keep in mind that ninety-five percent of it is all wrong, too."

"It's true about your name. Your mama was so outdone with you she started calling you AntiBelle and it stuck." AntiBelle had been in her life since she could remember, and she'd stepped in to pick up the slack when Ella Rae Sellers died. But as hard as AntiBelle tried, she went to her home each day, and Bronwyn was left alone in the big house with her father.

"That part is true." AntiBelle scooped up the empty plate and put it in the sink. "Come straight home from school today. Your daddy has a surprise for you."

Bronwyn's heart skipped. Could it be the thing she wanted most of all?

AntiBelle shook her head. "Don't get your hopes up. It isn't that kind of a surprise."

Bronwyn frowned. "What kind of surprise is it?"

"The kind you can't change and will just have to learn to live with. Now off to school and do me proud. Match yourself against my record." AntiBelle fingered the pack of cigarettes in her front shirt pocket. She always wore tropical floral prints, only cotton, with big marsupial pouch pockets. Killed the need for a purse, she said. She paired the shirts with skinny-legged jeans and bejeweled sandals in the summer and boots when the weather got cold.

"Not hard," Bronwyn said, hitching up her skirt to expose a little more thigh. "I'll try not to get expelled."

§

Turning down Suttie's invitation to ride to Jackson for an after-school shopping expedition had been hard, but Bronwyn had no choice. AntiBelle had told her to come straight home. Bronwyn found herself walking along the street from the high school to her home, kicking piles of dead leaves. Once she'd loved raking the sycamore leaves with her mother, laughing and jumping in them, scattering all the hard work and not caring. She'd loved autumn then. She'd been a child, of course, thrilled with anything her mother cooked up to do. Scruffing through the brittle pecan leaves on the sidewalk, she could almost touch those days. When she reached out wanting to bring them closer, they were gone, just like her mother.

Wilborn Pughes's chestnut tree, not yet denuded by the coming winter, shimmered deep gold in the slanting October light. It was nearly four o'clock, but the days were growing short. From somewhere in the neighborhood the smell of a wood fire came to her, dredging memories of roasting marshmallows and evenings rocking on the porch, sipping cocoa while her mother told stories. Some days she wondered if maybe she'd made up her mother. The memories were so sharp and clear, but Bronwyn could no longer remember her mother's face. The scent of her light perfume lingered, the sound of her voice, the clothes she wore—but her face was gone. Bronwyn walked faster.

Her house was in an older, established neighborhood of two-story brick homes, solid, perfectly landscaped. The gardener had planted a variety of mums at the lych-gate. Pumpkins were centered on either side of the brick columns that marked the entrance to Wellspring Manor. She hated that her house had a name. The other kids at school tormented her about it. At sixteen, she would be allowed to date, but she couldn't imagine a boy actually driving to Wellspring Manor to pick her up. Or meet her father. None of the sophomore boys were that brave.

She started down the long drive and stopped. Her father was home. She checked her phone. It was only 4:15. Her father never came home earlier than six, and more often than not it was closer to midnight. She wasn't fool enough to believe he was meeting with legal clients into the wee hours of the morning, but everyone lied to her, especially her father.

AntiBelle had said he had a surprise for her. For one stupid moment she'd thought it might be something for her. Maybe the car she'd asked to have for her sixteenth birthday. AntiBelle had disabused her of such fantasies, and a good thing too. No, her father's surprise was all about him, and she could easily guess what it was.

She stopped short, unable to force herself to go a step farther. Instead, she walked around the house and pulled her bicycle from the garage. The blue, white, and silver cruiser had been her mother's, an old fashioned bicycle for easy rides to Fontana Creek for picnics and swims. It had been a while since Bronwyn had ridden, but the tires were good. A few cobwebs spun through the spokes, but she ignored them. She dropped her book bag into the thick centipede grass but kept her phone, turning the ringer off. She pushed off with her left foot and began to pedal.

It took thirty minutes of hard riding to get to the cemetery. By the time she panted up the last hill, the golden tones had fled the sky. Peach streaks and hues of lavender and peacock tinted the westward horizon. Though the shadows were thickening and she was not the bravest of girls, she rode under the ornate wrought iron arch that named the cemetery. A long lane of trees canopied out the last light of day. When she cleared the shaded drive, the land of the dead sprawled in front of her. Many of the graves were marked with flat slabs. Plenty of others boasted ornate headstones with epitaphs and Bible verses. She slowed beside a blank-eyed angel that held a wreath of roses.

"Elizabeth Dewey, daughter of Saul and Liza, Death stole her spirit before the hand of time could touch her beauty" was engraved on the angel's pedestal. Beyond Elizabeth's grave the cemetery rolled downhill and climbed the far side. A fiery sunset touched white marble markers of crosses, columns, and cherubs with a fuchsia glow.

Rose Hill Cemetery was famous in its own way. Everybody who was anybody was buried there. Her mother was. For two years now. Bronwyn avoided that grave, though. She didn't owe her mother a cemetery visit—or anything else. Not at all, and besides, she was looking for someone else. She pedaled down the gravel paths, unsure how to find the final resting place of the King of the Gypsies. She hadn't thought this through. Surely there was someone to ask, but the cemetery, with night slipping toward her, had been yielded to the dead.

As she turned east, she noticed the first star, bright and unwinking, on the horizon. The old rhyme came to her and she whispered it, then spoke her wish aloud. There was no one to hear it, so it would still come true.

She rode, watching the star as she dipped into hollows and pumped up hills. When she topped a small rise, a man in jeans and flannel stepped from behind a mausoleum and into her path. She slammed on the brakes and almost hurtled over the handlebars in her effort to avoid hitting him.

"Be careful," he said, grabbing the handlebars to steady the bike. "You're gonna hurt yourself."

He'd frightened all of the words right out of her.

"I'm James. I work here. You look lost."

"King of the Gypsies." It was all she could think to say.

He nodded and then pointed but his right hand never left the handlebars of her bicycle. The directions he gave were easy. "Don't linger here. Night is coming. The dead won't hurt you, but there are others who might." He let go of the bike and walked down the path, his shoes crunching in the pebbles, the only sound except for the clear song of a hermit thrush from a nearby clump of oleanders.

The blackened tree line crowded the horizon. Magnolia leaves, thick and coarse, drank the light, absorbing it into the black silhouettes. Small groups of hardwoods, devoid of leaves, reached up as if to grasp the last sky colors. Bronwyn followed the man's directions and easily found the graves of Emil and Kelly Mitchell, King and Queen of the Gypsies.

Both graves were marked with large crosses, but the broken slab of Kelly Mitchell's grave was decorated with beads, fruits, bread, and photographs. Kelly Mitchell died in 1915, a woman of forty-seven.

Bronwyn picked up a photo of a young woman in her lacey wedding dress. The heavy frame was surrounded by a silver vine holding crystal lavender tear drops. The woman's dark hair framed her face in curls, and her dark eyes seemed haunted, yet content. Was she the Gypsy Queen? Bronwyn could only suppose. She replaced the photo and examined the other offerings: a necklace of what appeared to be carved bone, several strange coins, flowers, an apple, a pear, a cluster of radishes, slices of fresh bread. They were meant as gifts to Kelly Mitchell, Bronwyn could tell that much. In school they'd studied the embalming of the pharaohs and how great wealth was buried with them, along with food and slaves who were murdered so the great pharaoh would have them to attend his needs in the afterlife.

The last glimmer of light faded and Bronwyn remained kneeling by the grave. She couldn't see anything except the gravel path leading out of the cemetery. The stones picked up the starlight. She wasn't ready to leave yet. She had questions.

Her mother had run away with gypsies when she was fifteen. Why? Bronwyn listened to the beautiful song of the hermit thrush and tried to wrest an answer. She had an idea of her mother in her head, and at last her wish was fulfilled and she conjured a hazy face. She was the pretty blond woman who played touch football in the side yard on holidays. She wore coral lipstick and pale gray eye shadow that highlighted her blue eyes. Her name was Ella Rae, and she perfectly matched her clothes and accessorized and was a favorite of all Bronwyn's school friends. Everyone loved to spend the night at Bronwyn's house because Mrs. Sellers made it fun.

For a long moment she visualized her mother there, standing at the grave, in her favorite red sweater and black slacks. The wind ruffled her blond curls, so much like Bronwyn's. The faint lemony scent of her perfume came to Bronwyn on the ghost of a breeze.

"Why did you run away with the gypsies?" Bronwyn asked aloud.

"I wanted adventure." Ella Rae's smile was sad. "I wanted a new life."

"But you returned home."

"Yes."

"Would you still be alive if you hadn't come back?"

"That question doesn't have an answer."

"I can't go home and I don't know where to go. I want to go with the gypsies." Bronwyn looked up and realized she was alone. Her mother, if she'd ever really been there, was gone.

She checked her cell phone and saw the numerous calls from her father. Even AntiBelle had left messages. Bronwyn was in big trouble, no doubt. No one would believe that she'd been abducted by gypsies and managed to escape and find her way home. The bicycle was a dead giveaway.

Car lights punctured the darkness around her, and she stood, watching the vehicle slowly approach. Who would visit a cemetery at night, except for a girl who wanted her mother and didn't want to go home? It occurred to her that she should be afraid. Bad people roamed the world, and this could be one of them. But she didn't move. Maybe it was a Gypsy, come to visit the graves of the King and Queen. Maybe it would be her ticket to a new life, far away from Meridian.

The car, one Bronwyn finally recognized, crawled along the road, turning right and disappearing down a hill, only to reappear a moment later as the headlights angled up and then leveled out, revealing the path. It halted under the branches of a towering cedar tree not fifty yards away, and a woman got of the 1959 Cadillac Eldorado convertible.

"Bronnnn-wynnn!"

She recognized AntiBelle's gravelly voice. And she knew which grave AntiBelle had parked beside. Her mother's. AntiBelle went there every week to put fresh flowers on Ella Rae's grave. Bronwyn rose from the chilly ground and brushed the dead leaves and grass from her school skirt. Her legs were cold. She should have worn tights, but when she'd dressed for school, a cemetery visit hadn't been on the agenda.

"Bro-o-on-wynnn!"

"Coming." She didn't exactly yell, but illuminated by the car's lights, AntiBelle turned toward her. "I'm coming." Bronwyn picked up the bicycle and pushed it toward the car. It took her several minutes, but she got there.

AntiBelle's warm hands cupped her face. "Honey, your daddy is fit to be tied."

"I don't care. I'm not going home. Take me with you."

"Let's put the bicycle in the trunk. One advantage of driving this old tank is that there's plenty of trunk space." AntiBelle opened the car as she talked. Together they hefted the bicycle into it, turning the front wheel so it folded on itself. "Your daddy is always telling me this old Eldorado is a sin, that it burns too much gas, and hogs parking space, and other such unpleasant things, but I can put four dead bodies in the trunk, should the need ever arise."

Bronwyn wondered that her mother's best friend thought in such terms. Maybe if her mother had been more outspoken, less accommodating, things would have turned out differently. AntiBelle thought and said what she pleased. She did exactly what she wanted, even coming to the house each day to cook and check on Bronwyn. Bronwyn's father didn't like it, but he couldn't stop it. He didn't dare try.

Bronwyn got in the passenger seat and sat rigidly as AntiBelle drove her home. When they pulled in the drive, AntiBelle let the car coast to a stop. There were two police cars parked near the house. Bronwyn knew she was about to catch hell.

"Did you learn anything from the Gypsy royalty?" AntiBelle asked.

Bronwyn hesitated. At last, she asked. "If Mama had stayed with the gypsies, would she still be alive today?"

"There's no answer to that, Bronwyn. Your mother was a lovely woman who adored you. The two of you—I used to watch you together and though I never wanted children, sometimes I could taste how much I'd missed, not having a daughter of my own. The thing about life, you make your decisions and then you live those to the fullest. You put every ounce of life you can in them. You never think about how it might have been. That's a waste. I can tell you that your mother never squandered time with regrets."

"If she didn't regret, why'd she kill herself?"

"I have my theories about that, but I don't have any proof."

Bronwyn saw a commotion in the front yard. The exterior lights of the house bloomed and her father rushed out the front door and pounded down the drive. He still wore his shirt and tie. Behind him, a feminine silhouette appeared in the doorway. She knew who it was. Her father's legal secretary, Kylie. The woman her father had been screwing for three years.

"Will you tell me your theories?"

"Not today. But maybe one day. The only thing that really matters is that Ella Rae loved you more than anything."

Bronwyn snorted. "Right. She loved me so much she killed herself and left me all alone."

"Buck up, Bronwyn. There's always more to a story than meets the eye. Right now, your daddy needs to hear something that will smother that flame of fury he's about to unleash. What are you going to tell him?"

Bronwyn didn't have the energy to think up a lie. "The truth. That I went to see the King and Queen of the Gypsies."

AntiBelle smiled. "Your mama tell you to say that? It's perfect. Just don't tell him they're dead. Give no details. Hold firm to your story and ride out the storm. Never let anyone make you change your story, you hear me?"

"Is he going to marry Kylie?"

"Probably, but you're sixteen in two weeks. You can tough it out. You're always welcome at my house, and if you play your cards right and don't dig in your heels, things will go a lot easier. Your daddy can make your life hard or cushy. Go for cushy."

Her father was only fifteen yards away, his face mottled with anger.

Bronwyn could almost see the pulse in his temple in the bright car lights. She sucked in a breath and opened the car door.

"Where the hell have you been?" He grabbed her shoulder in a painful grip. "I've had the law looking for you. I found your book bag in the yard and no sign of you. Suttie said you walked home. Where have you been?" He shook her.

She wanted to cry, but she held it in. She glanced at AntiBelle who remained in the car. "I paid a visit to the King and Queen of the Gypsies."

He quit shaking her. "What foolishness is this? There aren't gypsies in Lauderdale County."

She shook free of him and straightened her shirt. "They told me my future, Daddy. What I should do to find happiness." She stepped away. "I didn't want to come home, but AntiBelle made me. You should be thanking her." She started down the driveway toward the house, then suddenly turned around.

"AntiBelle, what *is* your real name?" She'd never asked. There had been times AntiBelle had offered closeness, but she'd rebuffed her. Now she had a million questions, and in the coming days, she would ask them.

The low, deep chuckle came from the dark interior of the car. "It's Bronwyn. You were named after me. I begged her not to stick that moniker on you, but she was a stubborn woman."

"Thanks for the lift." Bronwyn stepped around her father and crunched down the drive. She could tolerate anything for two more years. Then high school would be behind her, and maybe she'd figure out something where she could change her name, like AntiBelle had done. Or maybe she really would run away with the gypsies. The future held endless possibilities.

Barbara Hamby

ODE TO MY SUMMER OF CHEKHOV

When I couldn't figure out how to write a story, I spent
        a summer reading Chekhov, at first taking notes,

but then just reading to let Chekhov invade my mind,
        which was laziness, but after a few years I seemed

to be able to write a sentence that didn't scream like an animal
        being slaughtered. But what else happened that summer?

Was that when I learned the trick with my neighbor's calico cat,
        a creature so pretty and aloof that it was hard not to beg

for her attention, but one day I was sick as Chekhov's bishop
        and lay down in the grass under our oak tree,

so I could watch the clouds passing above the giant limbs
        as if they had something to tell me about my own heart,

and she was there, pushing her little acorn head under my hand
        and I scratched her ears until we both went to sleep.

Or what that the summer I learned to make preserves, standing
        for hours over cauldrons of peaches like an alchemist

and stacking the jars of tomatoes and blueberries and figs
        and cherries in my pantry like a Russian peasant woman,

or was that the summer of the Chopin étude or the plague
        of tomatoes? How many times did I call my mother

that summer, thinking how to reach her, plotting like a spy
        or a Bolshevik infiltrator or a linguist trying to learn

her language—me whom she made from her own body? Now she's gone
        and I long for the mystery of her love, the cajoling

as of a reluctant lover, the fight–the fist of her words
        meeting flesh of my abdomen. How many times did I say

"yes" to her "no" and wish I could take her face in my hands
        and look into her eyes, that sea of my own days on earth.

George Held

LAURA BRIDGMAN AND THE MOUSE

> *I wad be laith to rin an' chase thee*
> *Wi' murd'ring pattle.*
> —"To a Mouse," by Robert Burns

In the confines of her chamber
At Perkins, Laura daydreams
Of flying out the window—
Then she hears the rustling
Of fur along the baseboard.

"O it's that mouse again," she
Exclaims, growing furious
To think of its temerity
Invading her familiar space
Like some nether Sam Howe

Before he met Julia Ward
And lost interest in Laura.
"O that dratted mouse," she
Says and spontaneously
Turns predatory.

Her acute hearing, like a bat's
Echolocation, homes in
On that "wee sleekit cowran
Tim'rous beastie" spared
By Mr. Burns's tolerance.

Miss Bridgman, with her best
Square-dancing form, takes steps
Left and right, forward but rarely
Back, tracking the mouse
Into a corner where it cowers.

The second sight of the blind
Empowers the young woman
To spring, with one shoe forward,
Upon the mouse and start stomping
The stuffing out of him, and how!

Barbara Henning

IN A CITY LIKE THIS

Everyone's on the go,
everyone but the man
sleeping beside the garbage,
his cheek on the cement,
a baseball hat over his face,
people stepping over him.
His sign: I'm a veteran.
Forty years after the U.S.
stopped spraying agent
orange in Vietnam jungles,
we're starting to clean up.
A full moon partly visible
through the trees. When
I climb into bed, my veteran
lover is sleeping in the chair.
I ask him if he's coming
to bed and he squints and
says, I know what I want.
When another person is stern
with me, my heart gets heavy.
Genny says, Yoga is a healing
art. Just by doing it, you
open blockages in the body.
There's always the possibility
of taking a seven-and-a-half
mile walk, lying flat with
pressurized inflatable cuffs,
hooked up to a heart monitor.
Inflate, deflate. Someday
we'll spray saltwater into the air
and make big soft salt clouds
to reflect dangerous sunlight
and reverse global warming.
I close my eyes and imagine
deep salutations to the sun.

Roald Hoffmann

THE DIFFERENCE BETWEEN ART AND SCIENCE

It's the land of the Slinky, warped mirrors,
the seemingly misfit gears of eccentric
motion. It's the modern science museum.
You would have to drop a crowbar on a gong
to hear it above decibels of ten-year-old
visitors. The masterpieces—Planck's quantum
hypothesis, the quinine synthesis—are missing.
Only the photos of the makers, the tangible,
billboards explaining the mystery of common sense.

In the hushed temple of high art one is moved
from the discreet space carved out by a Simone
Martini to the Master of the Urbino Annunciation.
It's the untouchable preserve of patrimony,
cautiously labelled for the farsighted, all
masterpieces, at least until deaccessioned.
But there it hangs, my Crivelli with a fly,
in the palace of unique resolutions, once done
waiting patiently to be done again, differently.

Randall Horton

Suspended, As

in the current's fabric of one's [self],

hanging from a tree, if not bodies,
leaves fluttering against night's rustic

sound: a chinook, a brittle *swoosh*—

down by the riverbed. call it virginal
alongside open-field: day & then

that frame: a cold shivering gentile

on the block, one heel gutter bound.
secreted inside a storefront's cleft

 a man drowned by gin's delirium,

maybe suspended reddish pixels
drawn up from dirt. say a [self] less

figure in a scream, another deferral

sleep walking while awake above
daffodil heads painted alabaster, but

what of the purple wisteria's blue,

the mockingbird's obbligato—
altering time if for a moment. if

a raven is stuck in the dark silence

of night: here everything returns
into another tunnel & then—:

Randall Horton

AS IF, UPON

exiting darkness begins the process
by which, of course, "I" dissolves

dim opaque, & a train whistling
by the last window to the right.

against plate-glass bubbled the cheek
but then oblique, as in—

pressed ever so silly dumb the night
vibrant & uptown folk trapped

in a maze of identity, boundaries
the cheek belongs to (us), or so

thinks our protagonist. no matter
totally recuses itself from living,

once was said, not sure of he nor she—:

looking up at a red tail comet stab
through darkness the young character

begins dream as manifest destiny.
there is departure in arrival.

say our protagonist is a little he

trapped in a little supposed frame.
say the frame walks the streets

in search of gender everywhere.

the fallacy willing the frame.
say the skin construction is dark

deepening the scene's melanin.

an idea.
let's call our protagonist human?

Ramona Hyman

GRACE'S STORY: FOR JIMMIE LEE JACKSON

February 26, 1965:

When Jesus caught up with Grace
She was sitting on the steps of the shack house
Broom stick resting on her lap
A bleeding cross around her neck
Her blood shot eyes were traveling up
Heaven met her half way
She whispers—Jesus

>*Did you know Jimmie Lee Jackson*
>*Your deacon at the St James Baptist Church*
>*Cager's grandson , Viola's boy*
>*Was shot down right there in Mack's Cafe*
>*Old Fowler stole the boy's life*
>*I'm marching in honor of Jimmie Lee Jackson*
>*Need to hug him healed in my head*

When Jesus met Grace
She was leaning on the broom
Cross hanging from her neck—dripping blood
She's walking to Selma on to Montgomery
For Jimmie Lee Jackson
Like Jesus walked on water

Julie Kane

FROG SONNET

I don't wear silver, I wear gold—but, still,
That little silver frog jumped out at me,
Estate sale ring that fit me perfectly
Although I don't like frogs and never will

(Their sliminess, their picklish shade of dill,
Their fate in kitchens—frequent amputees);
What caused that unintended shopping spree,
That need to own it? It was not free will.

You, too, struck something in me when we met,
Although my first impression was, "This guy's
A snake-oil salesman." I would not have bet
My prince would come in froggy-like disguise

Long after I'd found fairy tales absurd.
Fate's language is the image, not the word.

X. J. Kennedy

RUMMAGE SALE

Here are the dregs of bookshelves no one wants:
Book of the Month Club choices now refused,
The memoirs of some general we forget,
Labor-intensive cookbooks still unused—

The castoffs of a season of demeaning
Cleared from the house in time to shrilling peepers,
Eliminated by a brisk spring cleaning.
Bookbuyers these folks were, but not book-keepers.

I wonder at this thick tome's long descent,
Hacked out by one whose fame and sales were stellar,
Plummeted from the tower of success
To molder in a spiderwebbed best cellar.

Lissa Kiernan

ADAM & EVE ON A RAFT AND WRECK 'EM

I'm slinging eggs again—like a surly short-order cook:
potbellied, bestained apron, whiff of bacon
all about me. I should have given up long ago,

but try telling these ovaries who still seem to believe
they can go out on a Saturday night, throw pickle-
backs down and hear four bands play sludge-

punk, which sounds a little like *MITTELSCHMERZ*
would were it sonic. Like frogs & follicular swelling,
crows & fallopian contractions, blood-

hounds in the hay. The band's name?
Little Old Ladies. I am not making this up.
The lead singer wears Adidas and a duster,

pink and blue daisies on cheap thread-
barren cloth. The duster's all-important
patch-pockets sag and sway when he slings

his meaty man hands up and down the neck
of his electric. You just know she has a name
like Scarlett. Hemingway maintains

*THERE IS NOTHING to writing—all you do is sit down
at a typewriter and bleed.* O, luxury
of metaphor! Without figurative expression,

I have sat down and bled at my desk, stood up
and bled in the train. I have lain down
in a strange Paris bed, and bled and bled and bled.

So today, in the shower, when the blood comes
dark and fast as squid ink, I am suddenly so tired
of bleeding, so tired, period. I have wanted this

life for so long. I have wanted to birth something,
anything, which might allow me to linger
a while longer in a world where how fast

we are forgotten. I have wanted a life
that goes on long after breakfast, long past
the five o'clock shadow lengthens and greases

the grill cook's neck. Doc wrote me a script,
says there is a test I can take to find out
how many more? I secreted it in a drawer.

Amy King

LOVE, I'M NOT THE STONE

Silence creeps and goes blue, no
Black song in my voice rises to you.
Beat beat, the underlying
Is what's missing, gone is the holy.
At dawn you've matured into a cow.
Even the smallest of us can prick fire,
Can beat at waves, we shores
Are Magritte and his stone
Paintings, Sisyphean breaths of death in acrylic.
Love is for perfect people,
& there's just me in my chair of fibs
& a pastor with his ten foot church on a leash.
The rest is just the hole you feed to babies.
Moo, God says to the grifter in the mirror.
Why not giraffes on the day of rest instead?
Hit me with a train broadside.
Turn me into a version of your voice on steroids.
Burn the silence of colors gently,
Go goodnight uphill from this wound of plenty.

David Kirby

SLURRING AND CONTRADICTING

Oh, look, the couple at the next table have had too much
to drink: they started with frozen margaritas and washed
          their burrito supremes down with several pitchers of Dos
Equis and then finished up with shots of some god-awful
stuff that's not even from Mexico, and now they're slurring
          and, worse, contradicting each other: No, no, no, he says,
    you're wrong about tap water, not to mention vitamin D,
dairy products, fluoride, and she says, Don't you no, no,

          no me; you're wrong about everything. The Middle East?
Wrong. Global warming? Wrong again. Gun control?
               Delusional! The cause of and cure for Alzheimer's, AIDS,
          autism, amyotrophic lateral sclerosis? Wrong, wrong,
wrong, wrong! Or right, but for the wrong reasons. It would
               have been better if he and she had simply enjoyed a plate
          of roasted monkfish with fiddlehead ferns and trout roe
along with a nice Italian Falinghina, say, or a Bandol from

          France. Just one bottle. Though, as an excess of alcohol leads
demonstrably to loudness and sarcasm and, from there, to
               other and worse social pathologies, to wit, a kind of speech
          that is so badly mumbled as to be barely comprehensible to
the you who is mumbling it, much less your interlocutors,
               as well as the refutation of every word that emerges
          from your darling's rosebud mouth, a mouth that, a mere forty-five
minutes ago, seemed to utter not only the loftiest romantic

          sentiments but also a number of the wiser philosophical precepts
as well as no small number of trenchant observations on
               current events and, further, a mouth, that you had thoughts
          of pressing your lips to later in the evening, though that
is now no more a likelihood than is the prospect of a speedy cure
               for one or more of the terrible diseases abovementioned
          or lasting peace between the Israelis and their
implacable foes. Listen to them! Why, it is as though they've both just

read George Eliot's great novel *Middlemarch*, where it says,
"When the animals entered the Ark in pairs, one may imagine
            that allied species made much private remark on each other
and were tempted to think that so many forms feeding on
the same store of fodder were eminently superfluous,
            as tending to diminish the rations," that is, that knowledge
is finite in nature and must be cut into tiny pieces
and hoarded by each of us just as we hive up as many bites of food as we

can lest someone were to come along and snatch it from
us, make it their own. Once I took another man in my arms;
            I had just stepped into a public restroom when a fellow
threw his limbs into the air and collapsed in a seizure, so
I lay on him and wrapped my legs around his to keep him
            from hurting himself, which is when a third man walked in
and looked at us soberly, uncertain whether we
were fighting or cuddling. His knowledge was incomplete, you may say.

"Get help!" I cried, and he took off like a shot, and even
though two medics rushed in a few minutes later, I'll never
            know if he called them or someone else did, just as I'll
never know if he ever figured out what the two of us were
doing there on that floor, snorting and kicking. If he didn't,
            even better! He may have found himself at the beginning
of wisdom, as Melville surely did in this
description that Hawthorne's son Julian left of him: "He seemed

nervous and every few minutes would rise to open and then to shut
again the window opening on the courtyard. At first he was
            disinclined to talk, but finally he said several interesting
things, among which the most remarkable was that he was
convinced Hawthorne had all his life concealed some great secret,
            which would, were it known, explain all the mysteries
of his career." Reveal that secret, though, and no
Scarlet Letter, no *Blithedale Romance, Marble Faun, House of the*

Seven Gables—no Hawthorne, in a word. Let us not
seek to be right, then, to know more than others, and, worse,
            to confirm that we know that they know that we know more

than they do. Let us not browbeat, strong-arm, hector,
and bullyrag others, particularly those whom we adore
                    and wish to adore us in return. Let us not drink until
          we are hateful. Let us drink until we are merry,
and then let us put down our cups. Let us drink until we are silent.

Philip Kolin

LUCY

> *Lucy Mercer, Eleanor Roosevelt's social secretary,*
> *was FDR's secret mistress for years.*

Lucy, did FDR ever drape
his black Yalta cloak over
you, hoping he could fulfill
the promise that his libido worked?

It must have been awkward
working for Eleanor by day
wanting to love him by night.

Did you ever cross her name
off her stationary
to write your love notes to him?

I wonder if you and FDR
held each other's shadows
while she toured the world
in cold canteens and camps,
painting her bucktooth stiff smile
on Pathé newsreels.

Did you guide his shaking hand
to make it write straight
on all those letters to mothers
pleading to end the heartache in the Pacific?

The day Japan surrendered
so did you.

Yet all he bequeathed you
was a covert footnote in history.

Lucy, did he ever make you feel
like a woman who didn't need to come
under the cloak of a clearance
to visit his dreams?

Carolyn Kreiter-Foronda

O'KEEFFE'S DESERT TERRAIN, GHOST RANCH

I.
Simplify the details, she reminds
            herself, the clay road undulating
                        with heat, Chimney Rock

a stark cadence, a howl.
            Scanning the terrain, she watches
                        the Pedernal unveil clouds.

The slanted cap rock reaches out,
            beckons the artist to sketch
                        its frame as if it were a saint:

ancient, lordly, worthy of her ashes
            flung across its revered back.
                        A ghostly sunset appears—

eternal fire she emulates.
            Flames soar behind cliffs,
                        alter the throbbing design.

II.
Who cannot feel her presence woven
            into these wind-swept hills?
                        Today she simplifies

a tree, its limbs petrified, curled
            like antlers on a ram's head,
                        bleached bones

swallowed by a plush corridor
            of rays, by the steady sound
                        of hawks swooping

down to observe the desolate
     landscape she draws: flat-topped
        mountain stripped bare

as if washed by rain, the desert
     disrobed—like a lover
        seen for the first time.

Hank Lazer

N27P13

1/20/14

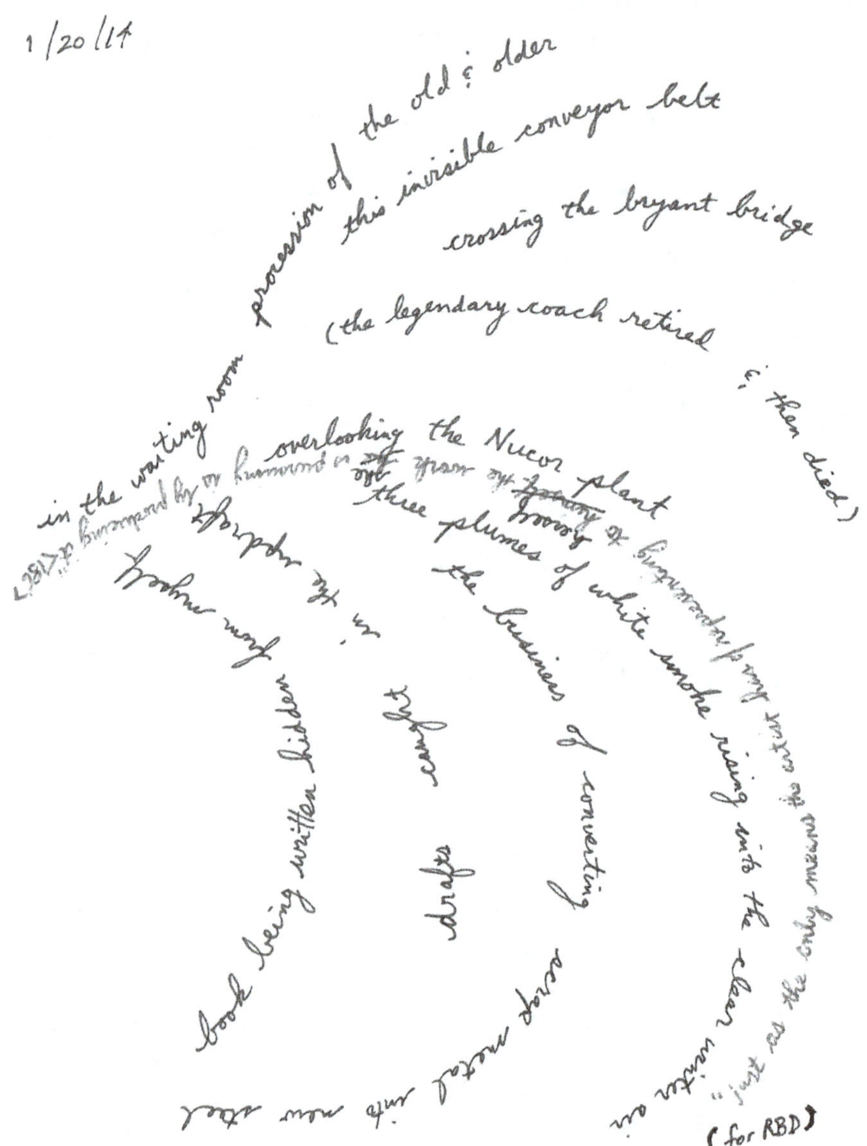

Hank Lazer

N27P31

2/15/14

"Being only exists for someone who is capable of stepping back from it and is thus himself

from here to there

a pointing toward

absolutely outside of being." <220>

are they messengers

call it angel or word

a single letter

from there

to here

Denise Low

AMARANTH

> *She examined the brilliant red amaranth.*
> —Leslie Marmon Silko

By June emerald forests spread
so vast they frighten Cortez.

They remain brilliant forty days.
After drought, leaves shrivel.

Brittle skeletons spike along ditches.
Seed clusters disperse.

The hard black beads measure soil,
communion drops of rain.

John C. Mannone

WHORLS OF OLEANDER AND SULFUR

After Starry Night by Vincent van Gogh

I absolutely want to paint a starry sky…
night is still more richly colored than the day
—Letter to his sister, Wilhelmina van Gogh
September 16, 1888

A conflation of memories: sailboats and
fishing vessels pastel against a stark sea,
the sharp edge of sun filleting horizon.

Boats clip through aquamarine, sails
dragging salt spray—rudder through
turbulence. Sparkles of sky are black

in the corner of the universe, light
constellations the village culled
from darkness, it swirls with absinthe

and cypress from recesses of his mind. Colors
flare the canvas, night blazing in oil, and stars
strung as pearls, shimmer
                              like waxlit candles
          dissolving

                into   spirals
          of currents   running through
the deep   black   Rhone

Damon Marbut

PROGENY

She is still driving home from San Diego,
exhausted by the lie that life had gone her way,
the expectation still packed somehow
in the trunk, in a suitcase,

or it had climbed on its own
into a wheel and spun itself back to Alabama and,
once she was touched by the first recognizable hand,
squeezed into the nearest layer of her skin
and bore down to grow. I cringe at my body
being that kind of tomb, that burying place
for stale cigarettes still wanting to burn,
lying unlit in a pile of what it has molted,
what it has given and lost.

Before the new decade broke,
I appeared to meet her gods
who looked me up and down quizzically
when she came from in between earthquakes,
found an empty space and lay me to puncture the floor,
set root, uproot, pull out of her and go.

Michael Martone

THE OFFICER OF THE DECK ABOARD USS PHILIPPINE SEA (CG 58) DEPLOYED, THE ATLANTIC OCEAN OFF MAYPORT, FLORIDA, CALLS ALL HANDS TO BURY THE DEAD

All stop! We don't often ship bodies. Norfolk's the usual departure port. This sailor's special. No GPS. Sextant. For this spot, I'll shoot the sun.

Michael Martone

An Engineering Technician of the NanoFab Operations Group at the Center for Nanoscale Science and Technology of the National Institute of Standards and Technology in Gaithersburg, Maryland, Attempts DNA Origami

Adenine/Thymine & Guanine/Cytosine. One long scaffold strand folded/folded/folded/folded/folded/folded/folded. How many folds, in half, before the half cannot be folded again?

Carlo Matos

TRIAL 17: 01/4/93

The snow brackens and is gone
without so much as a drip in the palm.
Big Foot runs amok in the forest,
still a genius at blurring his tracks.
The lost boys are in Paracas, or at least their skulls are.
And the Illuminati have sore and calloused hands
from pulling on their strings too hard.
They are in possession of the last book
written in tardigrade,
which must be found and destroyed,
drowned in the dead water that eats
the cataract glow of the bog-sun,
the dun touch of the hornet-moon,
the relaxing whistle of the ghost trains
crisscrossing the still-young earth.

Peter Meinke

ARS LONGA, VITA BREVIS

Now that I've reached the age
when I stumble up the stage
for some job-concluding pin
every evening out's a chore
Looking forward to my gin
I think with resigned regret
as I trip the final step
my *vita*'s not so *brevis* any more

Mortúus my youthful storms
all melancholy gone
those clouds are stacked away
on soundtracks of Marianne
and Eleanor Rigby dreams
I remember a ribbon on the floor
but what were my girl friends' names?
My sweetheart isn't *Mavis* anymore

America rolls like a pig
in dirty oil and gore
My country my pig I shout
to the stars whose blinking snouts
and planetary snuffles
uproot the universe
as they gather galactic truffles . . .
My *mentis* isn't *compos* any more

Looking around the world
why do I feel so gay
when I'm not gay at all
A martini's not strong enough
to block the world's fat fist
Is that what the olive's for
and the lemon's bitter twist?

My *gravitas* curls groveling on the floor

I dream of my old aunts still
bending over their cards
Nana and Lizzie and Lil
They pressed me against their hearts
I could hardly get my breath
Then they shooed me out the door
to my certain death:
My *vita*'s not so *brevis* any more

Teal Mims

THE LONG MILE: A MEASURE OF COMBAT

The Vietnam Veterans Memorial stretches for 493.5 feet.

If a similar memorial were constructed for World War II soldiers, it would be 3,560.5 feet (or 0.67 mile).

If a similar memorial were constructed for World War I soldiers, it would be 40, 103.5 feet (or 7.6 miles).

The Civil War memorial would be 5, 252 feet (or 1 mile).

These figures are just for United States Veterans.

Caryn Mirriam-Goldberg

PREVERNAL

The dogs stop. The deer
over the loop of the field
pause. The highway rising west
clears. I wait. Let my breath make itself
visible. Count the turkeys frozen
against the cedars or mid-field
between woods and prairie.
The wheel of the season waits too,
then rolls toward its next click.
Time to go closer to what's ready
to bud out, just last week, milk-deep in snow.

When the world resumes in birds
and greening trail, all on the verge
crossed over. Meets or doesn't meet
at the other side where dreams stand
on all four new legs, then jolt into steps
before considering the weight of landing.

Underground, rivers thread their long fingers
toward the coming length of days.
Overhead, the old flock returns,
drifting down to the tops of everything.

Robert Morgan

THE CALM

When Daddy said he'd shoot me if I didn't leave him alone I had to make an impossible choice: let him get sicker still, or risk being killed myself. He had the pistol in bed with him and was so mad he might well have used it. And he had a bottle of vodka too; in fact, he had several bottles on the night stand beside the bed. It was so dark in the bedroom I couldn't really count the bottles. He probably had others too, under the bed or in the closet. The Mexicans who worked for him in the fields brought him the liquor when I wasn't around and there didn't seem to be any way to stop it. "I love you, Daddy," I said. "And I think you should go to the hospital."

"You leave me where I am," he said. "Touch me and I'll kill you."

"Just want to help."

"You can help me by leaving me alone." Daddy laid the .44 magnum on the covers in front of him.

Daddy had always been bad to drink, especially on weekends and holidays. He and his buddies would get a six-pack or two and drive around in their pickup trucks and drink. And he liked to go down to South Carolina and buy white lightning before there was an ABC store in Hendersonville. After that, he could get all the legal liquor he wanted just by driving to town. When I was a boy, I cringed to see him come home drunk, hollering at Mama and throwing things around. And then after Mama left him and took my sister Mary to live with her folks down at Tryon, Daddy drank even more. I stayed with Grandpa and Grandma most of the time. And I pretended not to be embarrassed when Daddy got arrested for DWI and his name was in the paper and my friends at school would tease me. "Your daddy is famous," they'd say and laugh, and I would laugh loudest. Grandpa would be so mad at Daddy after he was arrested he wouldn't even talk to him. When they were watching television and Daddy would sit down on the couch, Grandpa would go out and sit in his car and listen to the radio. During election time, Daddy made fun of Grandpa for being a Democrat. Daddy and Grandma were Republicans. But when things really got bad for Daddy was after he was diagnosed with arthritis. I don't know if it was the bean dust that caused it, or the drinking, or something else.

But after he turned forty-five, he got these awful pains in his joints and swelling that wouldn't go away. Pain medicine didn't do much good for long, and his joints hurt so bad it was hard to move. He got too stiff all over to work much, and he couldn't sleep either. That's when he started drinking on weekday nights, and then in the daytime, too. The doctor in Asheville said there was a treatment with gold that might help him, though he'd have to go down to Duke for that. But the gold could have bad side effects too. Some people had even died when they took the gold treatment. Even so it was his best hope. The doctor gave Daddy a brochure that described the gold therapy, and he showed it around to people and asked their advice. But the side effects scared Daddy, and instead of going down to Duke, he just drank more.

About the same time, Grandpa died of a heart attack. It was a surprise to us, no warning at all. Grandpa just stopped his tractor in the field and got down saying he didn't feel good. He dropped to the ground right at my feet by a bag of fertilizer, and I tried to wake him up, but he was already gone. He was laying right there beside me, but he was gone. Though he'd quarreled and cussed Grandpa, Daddy took his death the hardest. Grandma and I grieved, but we grieved quietly. Daddy cried at the funeral, and he kissed Grandpa on the lips in the coffin. And he sobbed up at the graveyard too like he couldn't help himself. And then after the funeral it was like Daddy got mad that Grandpa was gone. Grandpa had always run the farm and looked after business. Now Daddy would have to keep up with things in spite of his arthritis and his drinking. "Human life don't mean nothing," Daddy said. "You're born and live and die just like that, and it don't mean a thing." Daddy bought Grandpa the most expensive tombstone he could find, and he brooded for months. And he cussed the preacher when he came by to visit. "Don't talk to me about no heaven," Daddy said. "I'd rather listen to my hound dogs holler after a possum or coon than hear a sermon." Grandma would try to stop Daddy from drinking. She'd try to talk to Daddy the way Grandpa had. "Throw that bottle away or I'll throw it out for you," she'd say. But Daddy would just ignore her, or he'd snarl, "Don't nobody touch my medicine," for he called vodka his medicine. I'd gone off to North Carolina State to study agriculture, and every summer I came back to work on the farm. It's a good thing I did for Daddy was drinking so much he couldn't really look after the Mexican work crews or the equipment or bookkeeping. Grandma did all she could, but I had to keep track of the payroll, carrying produce to market, keeping machinery repaired. Daddy would sit in his truck watching us work and sipping from his bottle. After the arthritis got worse, Daddy didn't go to the field anymore. He'd drive down to the store and sit on a bench, or drive around in his truck with one of his buddies. They'd go up on Pinnacle and sit and drink and look down on the county spread out below them. And sometimes they'd drive to bars in Greenville or Atlanta. But as the arthritis got worse he didn't even do that. Mostly he just stayed at home and nursed himself with a bottle.

After Daddy threatened me with the pistol I stayed away that day. The Mexican crews were stretching wire in the bean fields down on Gap Creek and I had to be there anyway. And then I had to run to town to get more wire for them to stretch the next day. By the time I returned to the house it was near dark. When I walked into the living room and turned on the light I saw Daddy laying on the couch. He'd passed out holding a bottle to his chest, and the pistol had fallen to the floor. I thought I would hide the pistol before carrying him to the bedroom. But when I reached down for the gun, his hand shot off his chest and grabbed my wrist. "Don't you touch that," he said. The vodka bottle fell to the floor, and he let it go and took the pistol instead. "You need to go to bed," I said.

"Can't you goddamn leave me alone?" Daddy said.

"You need a doctor." "You call a doctor and I'll blow your damn college brains out," Daddy said.

"I'll just carry you to the bedroom."

"I can walk," Daddy said.

I stepped back and he tried to sit up. He held the gun in his right hand and pushed himself with his left. But he was too weak or drunk to raise himself. And I could see the pain in his face. He winced with the force of the pain. He lifted himself a little and then fell back. I reached to help him, but he waved me away with the .44 magnum. There were tears in his eyes. When Daddy fell back on the couch, he tried one more time to raise himself and failed. He started to sob and turned his face away to the back of the couch.

"Don't call the goddamn ambulance," he said. "I won't, but I have to put you to bed."

It was all I could do to lift him off the couch. He was dead, drunken weight. Once I got him in my arms, I almost tripped over the bottle which rolled on the floor. Walking carefully, I carried him into the dark bedroom and laid him on the bed. He was still crying as I wrapped the covers around him. "Can I get you something to eat?" I said. "You need to eat."

"Get out of here," he said.

It would not be fair to say that Daddy always avoided work. It's true that when tedious things like tying bean strings or hoeing corn had to be done, he always found something else to do. Back before we had Mexican hands, we, all of us, had to work in the fields, Mama and Mary, Grandma and Grandpa. Daddy would drive us to the field in the morning and say he had to go after something, more poles or string or fuel for the tractor. And he'd go to the store and drink Co- Colas and talk to his buddies until it was dinner time. And then he'd bring us hotdogs and drinks and candy bars and peanuts to eat before he disappeared again. But what Daddy liked to do, the work he enjoyed, was anything to do with machines. Whether it was oiling a planter or fixing a posthole digger, he'd let nobody else touch it. He seemed to have a natural talent for machines and tools. And what he preferred more than anything else was driving the tractor, any kind of tractor, from a garden tractor to a Farmall Cub. But it was the big diesel tractor he loved most. In the spring, he could hardly wait to get it cranked up again, blowing out blue smoke and winter farts, driving it like a prancing horse down to the bottomland along the river. Sinking plow blades into the winter stubble, he turned the moist soil two big ropes at a time. Sometimes he liked to plow at night and sing so loud you could hear his voice over the roar of the diesel. Round and round the field he went, more times than a driver at the Daytona 500. By morning, the field was turned over all new and looked like fresh corduroy. Daddy had a knack with mechanical things. Even when drinking, he could fix anything, lawn mower motor or a gearbox. Anything made out of metal with an engine delighted him. He could start a chainsaw when nobody else could. He said motors ran on gasoline or diesel the way he ran on vodka.

I don't know if Grandma called the preacher or if he just stopped by the house the following afternoon. But when I came in from work, there was a Buick in the driveway and, in the living room, there was the preacher talking to Grandma. Preacher Bob looked and talked like a car salesman. In fact, he had once been a car salesman in Greenville. "Brother Ray," he said and shook my hand. "I've come by to see your daddy."

"I don't think he's well enough to see anybody," I said. We never mentioned Daddy's drinking to anybody outside the family.

"Perhaps I could just pray with him," Preacher Bob said. "A short prayer might do him good." I knew it was impolite to disagree with the preacher or try to turn him away. But I didn't want anybody to see Daddy in the shape he was in. And I certainly didn't want Daddy to point his pistol at the preacher or maybe even try to shoot him.

"Uh, maybe another time," I said.

"A prayer might ease his mind," Preacher Bob said.

Now, Daddy hadn't been to church in years, and he had a special scorn for preachers. The last person I wanted there was Preacher Bob. But while I was thinking about what to say, Grandma told the preacher, "You go on in and say a few words."

It was dark in the bedroom, and as we shuffled in, Grandma flicked on the light. Daddy must have been sleeping, but he opened his eyes and winced at the glare. "How are you, Brother Howard?" Preacher Bob said. "I dropped in to see about you."

My stomach felt like it was full of sharp-edged rocks. I knew I was an idiot for letting this scene happen.

"Who are you?" Daddy said.

"I'm Preacher Bob, the pastor. Can I offer up a prayer for you?"

"Is this a hospital?" Daddy said, looking around at me and Grandma.

"You're at home," I said.

"I just want to offer up a prayer," Preacher Bob said.

Daddy's hand came from under the covers, holding the .44 magnum. His arm was so weak the gun trembled. "Get your praying ass out of here," he said.

Preacher Bob reached out his hand like he was protecting himself, but he backed toward the door. We followed him into the living room. "I will pray for him," Preacher Bob said and slipped out the front door.

Grandma fixed soup and cornbread that evening, and as we sat at the table in the kitchen, I pondered what could be done. If I could get the pistol away from Daddy, I could call the ambulance and take him to the hospital. It would be the only way to save him. That was my moral duty and possibly my legal duty, too. It would be against all his wishes. I didn't know exactly what the right thing to do was, and there was nobody to help me. Did Daddy have a right to die any way he wanted to? What was my ultimate responsibility? Was Daddy in his right mind enough to know what he was doing? Was I guilty already for not taking the pistol away from him? By the time I finished the soup, I was determined to get the pistol away from him and call the ambulance. There was no use to call the ambulance until the .44 magnum was out of his hands. If I didn't get Daddy to the doctor, I'd blame myself for the rest of my life. You don't really have a choice, I told myself. I'd have to take the gun and somehow the rest would fall into place. But I didn't want to get shot myself. In his pain, Daddy was a light sleeper. It would be almost impossible to slip up on him, and even if I did, the pistol would be in his hand. Soon as I touched the gun, he'd wake up and point it at me. I was just going to have to take my chance, grab the pistol from Daddy, and hope he wouldn't shoot me. For I thought he didn't really want to hurt me. It was a risk I had to take.

"I'm going to get the pistol," I said to Grandma.

"Don't do that," she said. She was so embarrassed by the preacher's visit she'd hardly said anything through supper.

"It's the only way," I said. My plan was to slip into the bedroom and put my hand on Daddy's hand before he knew what I was doing. I'd jerk the gun away and throw it as far as I could before he realized what was happening. Then when he was unarmed I'd hold him down and yell to Grandma to call 911. Sick as Daddy was I could hold him there until the first responders arrived. I was so tense I hardly breathed as I approached the bedroom. I stopped at the door to listen but heard nothing. Are you making the worst mistake of your life? I asked myself. But I'd made up my mind, and there was nothing to do but go through with it. Stepping quietly as I could, I hurried to the bed and put my hand where I thought Daddy's hand would be under the covers. Sure enough, I felt the barrel of the pistol and gripped it hard. But there was no resistance. The .44 magnum came loose in my hand, and I flung it toward the door. I expected Daddy to grab me or hit me, but he was still.

Mary Murphy

PENCILS

Legless on a plank with wheels, he claims the corner of Government and Royal Streets as his own. A tin can with the remnants of a label sits on the sidewalk before him. Bright yellow pencils with orange erasers stand above the rim. My mother stops and asks for three, and places her hand on my left shoulder—lightly squeezing, the secret signal not to stare…but I do. Handing him the bills, I notice the black pants legs folded over and secured with large safety pins, the torn and dirty cream and blue checkered shirt, and a stubbled and unsmiling face that is a tangle of wrinkles. I watch as the spotless hand holds out sharpened pencils, hear him say: "Don't be scared little girl. They're not dirty."

Janet Passehl

DEAR ROWBOAT,

This depression is where the man drowned the day his dog wandered home.

Dear rowboat, the flag shimmies in the foreground, shrouds around its pole. Sarah will buy this place when she wins the lottery, if I don't. You are not the ghost ship, hardly, the one we watched last night, drifting. I'm so sorry about Don, but anyway I put lipstick on this morning like always. Simply said, there's no substitute for a well-defined pair of lips.

The *chhht chhht* of Sarah's broom on the boards sounds like "cheat cheat," but this I will never do. Not as long as the horizon stays well away, out there where some god placed it. "Despair despair," mimics no activity I can name. There is no time so quiet as high tide. Bodies are gone, heads glide and sip the silver-blue. I meant, dear rowboat, to write about a river, but now I fear this is the Ocean.

P.T. Paul

CONFESSIONS OF A STAR CATCHER

I thought they were baby stars,
the way they climbed the damp blanket of night
upward from the magnolia tree,
baby stars that had just gotten their wings
and had to strengthen them low to the ground
before leaving for the cosmos.

Carl Sagan said we were "star stuff,"
that EVERYTHING was "star stuff,"
us and everything having evolved
on what was surely some other child's star
who stared into the same black from a backyard
billions and billions of miles away.

Oh, I pretended to catch them,
when given a Mason jar by some helpful adult
who wisely knew what baby stars were really for.
But I would never quite seal the deal,
and stumbled and bumbled
until they couldn't bear to watch me anymore
and finally decided that maybe
I wasn't meant to be a star catcher.

Other children proudly showed me their glowing jars,
bragged about their prowess,
until the excitement of catching stars wore off
and they left their jars where the lids
could mysteriously become loose enough to fall off.

Unfortunately, I was sometimes too late,
and all that was left was a smidgen of wings,
a smudge of "star stuff" that smeared my fingers,
but I still had to fling what was left into the air,
just in case a tiny soul needed a lift heavenward.

Marjorie Perloff

WHITMAN IN THE NEW CENTURY

Will we stroll dreaming of the lost America of love past blue
automobiles in driveways, home to our silent cottage?
–Allen Ginsberg, "A Supermarket in California" (1955)

The "lost America of love" Ginsberg speaks of so nostalgically here has changed beyond recognition in the half-century since Ginsberg, one of the most important of Whitman's heirs, wrote these words. For the great Modernists from Ezra Pound, Hart Crane and William Carlos Williams, to Charles Olson, Robert Duncan, and the Beats, Whitman was the Great American Poet—a visionary who was also a populist, a truly democratic poet who celebrated men and women from all walks of life and yet had, for himself, a predilection for male "comrades," a maker of beautifully crafted lyric, whose long Biblical free-verse lines were carefully wrought, their richly varied diction orchestrated by anaphora and alliteration.

The past few decades, however, have witnessed a slow but subtle change: in academe, Whitman continues to be revered and studied, but for the poets of the 21st Century, he has become largely irrelevant. Consider the evidence provided by two books that have tried to keep up the Whitmania of mid-century: *Walt Whitman: The Measure of his Song*, edited by Jim Perlman, Ed Folsom & Dan Campion for the small Holy Cow Press in 1981 and the recent *Visiting Walt: Poems Inspired by the Life and Work of Walt Whitman*, edited by Sheil Coghill and Thom Tammaro for the University of Iowa Press in 2003.

The former collection is the brainchild of the Whitman critic Ed Folsom, working with two former students from his University of Iowa seminar in 1980. "So palpable is Whitman's presence," writes Folsom in his Introduction (xxi), "that it is difficult for an American poet to define himself or herself without direct reference to him." This was true in the earlier decades of the century: even Wallace Stevens, a poet not given to Whitmanian effusions, had begun "Like Decorations in a Nigger Cemetery" with the lines:

> In the far South the sun of autumn is passing
> Like Walt Whitman walking along a ruddy shore.
> He is singing and chanting the things that are part of him,

The worlds that were and will be, death and day.
Nothing is final, he chants. No man shall see the end.
His beard is of fire and his staff is a leaping flame.

(Perlman p. 93)

Stevens's Whitman is not the celebrant of "Crossing Brooklyn Ferry" but the dark Whitman of "Out of the Cradle Endlessly Rocking" and "As I Ebb'd with the Ocean of Life," the poet who knows and confronts Death. "Come lovely and soothing death": these words have been celebrated by such poets of the 1960s as James Wright (*Measure* 166), who praised Whitman's "intelligence, his courage, his supremely delicate imagination" (175). In 1963, Theodore Roethke took a similar line in "The Abyss":

> Be with me, Whitman, maker of catalogues
> For the world invades me again,
> And once more the tongues begin babbling.
> And the terrible hunger for objects quails me. . . .
> For I have moved closer to death, lived with death. . . . (180)

But already in those "deep image" poets Roethke and James Wright, one senses a certain *embarrassment* vis-à-vis Whitman's exuberant and hyperbolic mode, so different from Wright's own understated and oblique short lyrics. Then, too, there is the matter of Whitman's homosexuality, quite unmistakable in such poems from *Calamus* as "Wherever You Are Holding Me Now In Hand," which contains lines like:

> Or if you will, thrusting me beneath your clothing,
> Where I may feel the throbs of your heart or rest upon your hip,
> Carry me where you go forth over land or sea. . . .[i]

Mainstream poets of mid-century like Robert Lowell and John Berryman were ill at ease with this material; it was left to the gay poets of the time to carry on the tradition. A notable—and little known—example is that of Ronald Johnson, two of whose beautiful "Letters to Walt Whitman" are included in the Perlman anthology (185-86). Here is the first section of V:

Earth my likeness

I, too, have plucked a stalk of grass
from your ample prairie, Walt,
& have savored whole fields of a summer's hay in it—

I have known your Appalachian length, the heights
of your Sierra
--I have unearthed the roots of calamus
you left at the margin

of many, hidden ponds,
& have exchanged it with the few, select
lovers.

Johnson understands Whitman, but he doesn't try to write in his mode.
Rather, being a visual poet, who has been heavily influenced by Concrete
poetry, he recharges Whitman's language, fragmenting his lines so as to
produce a more intimate, quiet tone than Whitman's own. Johnson's
landscape is the Kansas prairie, and in "Letters XI," he focuses on the
reverse side of the ecstatic merger with the earth depicted in V:

All is Oz.

The dusty cottonwoods, by the creek,
rustle an Emerald City.

And the mystic, immemorial city
is rooted in earth.
All is Oz & inextricable.

bound up in the unquenchable flames of double suns.
(185-86)

Kansas is both "ample prairie" and the dreary commercial world
of Emerald City in *The Wizard of Oz*. Whitman, so Johnson implies,
understood both sides of this equation perfectly: witness "The Sleepers"
or "As I Ebb'd with the Ocean of Life."

In a more oblique fashion, Frank O'Hara honors Whitman in poems like his 1956 "In Memory of My Feelings":

> Beneath these lives
> the ardent lover of history hides,
>
>   tongue out
> leaving a globe of spit on a taut spear of grass[ii]

The "lives" in question are those of characters from history, fiction, and film, whose identity the poet takes on so as to protect and mask his own secret self. The "taut spear of grass," as Whitman knew it, now has a "globe of spit" on it. But comic and absurd as is the sequence that follows, O'Hara's cataloguing is clearly derived from Whitman, beginning with the acknowledgement of the "Grace / to be born and live as variously as possible." Now come the "sordid identifications":

> I am a Hittite in love with a horse. I don't know what blood's
> in me. I feel like an African prince I am a girl walking downstairs
> in a red pleated dress with heels I am a champion taking a fall
> I am a jockey with a sprained ass-hole I am the light mist
>   in which a face appears
> and it is another face of blonde. I am a baboon eating a banana
> I am a dictator looking at his wife I am a doctor eating a child
> and the child's mother smiling I am a Chinaman climbing a mountain
> I am a child smelling his father's underwear I am an Indian
> Sleeping on a scalp
>   And my pony is stamping in the birches,
>   And I've just caught sight of the *Nina*, the *Pinta* and the *Santa Maria*.
>   What land is this, so free?   (O'Hara, 256)

This is usually taken to be a burlesque of the idealistic cataloguing of *Song of Myself*, O'Hara's identifications, as with the girl in the red pleated dress or with the champion taking a fall, being drawn from the Hollywood films of his day in what is hardly a participation in some larger Unity of Being. Yet the variety of reference has something of Whitman's exhilaration, and when we come to Columbus's three ships and the poignant question, "What land is this, so free?", one senses that, like Whitman, O'Hara is quite aware of the freedom he has been accorded. The child smelling his father's underwear, the Indian sleeping on a scalp—these are, however skewed toward burlesque, Whitmanian properties.

But as the *fin de siècle* approached, the celebratory note became increasingly fainter. By 1979, David Ignatow could declare, "I see my relationship to Whitman as that of a dissident son to an over-demanding father. He demands, as he does of himself, total allegiance to a transcendental version of existence. I can't see it, especially not on his terms" (Perlman 178). Transcendence! There was the rub. Louis Simpson, who praises Whitman's irregular meters and forms, his images of cavalry crossing a ford and a "Muse install'd amid the kitchenware," remarks that Whitman's "whooping it up over the chest-expansion of the United States didn't do a thing for me. His wish for young men to throw their arms about his neck struck me as incomprehensible. I was put off by his use of big-sounding words or French words." And Simpson cites the lines, "I see the Brazilian vaquero, / I see the Bolivian ascending mount Sorata," commenting that "I don't see how anyone could ever read these passages in Whitman with pleasure" (257).

An even more severe evaluation is that of Robert Bly, whose "What Whitman Did Not Give us" (1981) lists seven areas in which Whitman is deficient: "care for male masters, the problems of pain, the emphasis on audience, care for small sounds, care for pauses, the problem of observation vs. participation, and the question of whether private or public speech is appropriate to poetry" (322). By "care for male masters," Bly is referring to Whitman's lack of deference to precursors. Thoreau, Bly argues, looked up to Emerson; Rilke regularly cited Hölderlin, Goethe, and Baudelaire, but Whitman writes as if he is somehow self-created. He does not, moreover (stricture #2) understand human pain: for Whitman, "the way to solve pain," Bly explains disparagingly, "is to transcend pain, simply declare yourself healthy" (324). As for sound, there are too many "unstressed syllables," too many function words—articles, prepositions, conjunctions—that dampen the intensity of a given poem. Ignoring the use of pause, essential to the poetic line and stanza, Whitman, Bly feels, fails to make the crucial distinction between public and private speech and is thus a problematic influence for his followers (332).

Bly himself wrote a carefully condensed imagist lyric that would have been anathema to Whitman. American poetry in the 1970s had become curiously unambitious. It was the age of the Creative Writing

Workshop, and poets were reluctant to take risks. Then, too, it was the time of first-stage feminist poetry—a poetry unlikely to respond to what it took to be Whitman's masculine and all-encompassing ego. But the decisive turn against Whitman came, perhaps most fully, with the advent of Language Poetry in the mid-1980s. True, Ron Silliman's *Tjanting* and other long prose works of the period are Whitmanian in their desire to leave nothing out, their attempt to *render* the minute details of life in all their plenitude. But the obliquity of Emily Dickinson now replaced the seeming overstatement of Whitman, and Dickinson's fierce separateness from her culture appealed especially to the women poets of the Language movement. You will not find, in the critical essays that comprise, say, Lyn Hejinian's *The Language of Inquiry*, Joan Retallack's *The Poethical Wager*, or Rosmarie Waldrop's *Dissonance* (*if you are interested*), so much as a mention of Whitman. Susan Howe, whose work is squarely centered on the conflicts of the American ethos, from the Frontier and Transcendentalists to Emily Dickinson, speaks of Whitman *en passant*, for example in her elegiac memorial piece on the great Whitmanian critic F. O. Matthiessen in *The Birth-mark* (1991). But her own poetry, which repeatedly draws on Dickinson, does not place itself in the Whitman tradition.

Indeed, the identification with Whitman so common earlier in the twentieth century is replaced, in the twenty-first, by the polite and somewhat bland respect one meets in the poems that comprise *Visiting Walt*. A major portion of the one-hundred poems culled by Coghill and Tammann in their anthology pay overt homage to Whitman without being able, seriously or even parodically, to capture his rhythms or his voice. Erica Jong, for example, has a poem called "Testament (Or, Homage to Walt Whitman)," which begins:

> I, Erica Jong, in the midst of my life,
> > having had two parents, two sisters,
> > two husbands, two books of poems
> > & three decades of pain. . . .   (114)

and proceeds via such flat generalization as "Doom is cheap," "Gloom is cheap" to the exhortation:

> if we can be sufficient to ourselves,
> > we need feel no entangling webs

> The love root will germinate. (118)

Or again, Daniel Hoffman has a clumsy poem called "Crossing Walt Whitman Bridge" (the bridge that connects New Jersey to Pennsylvania), which opens:

> Walt, my old classmates who write poems
> Have written poems to you.
> They find you, old fruit,
>
> In the supermarket, California;
> They hear you speaking from the brazen mouth
> Of your statue on Bear Mountain. . . . (88)

And so it goes, flat-footedly, from poem after poem, the whole compendium convincing us of nothing so much as that Whitman's spirit seems, at least for the moment, to have been lost. "Whitman": today the name conjures of the "special" edition of *Leaves of Grass*, now reduced to a book of moral uplift, that Bill Clinton gave as a gift to Monica Lewinsky.

But there are signs that this situation is once again changing. Younger performance poets like Christian Bök and Caroline Bergvall, are foregrounding the prominence of rhythm and sound structure—areas where Whitman, Robert Bly's strictures notwithstanding, stands supreme. Let me close with the first five lines of one of Whitman's great poems:

> As I ebb'd with the ocean of life,
> As I wended the shores I know,
> As I walk'd where the ripples continually wash you Paumanok,
> Where they rustle up hoarse and sibilant,
> Where the fierce old mother endlessly cries for her castaways....
>
> (*Leaves of Grass*, 253)

The anapests of the first few lines mime the steady wave motion of the water, but no sooner is that rhythm established than it is countered by the harshness of "continually wash you Paumanok." The hissing of line 4 now culminates in what must be one of the most amazing lines in American poetry, its opening anapest, "Where the fierce," colliding with two stressed syllables in "óld mother," only to be followed by three dactyls, that modulate sibilants and voiceless stops so as to provide us with a sonic equivalent of the ocean's terrible cry, its deathcall to the poet. The emerging Whitman, I predict will not be the poet who "celebrates" himself, but the elegiac Whitman of poems like this one—a Whitman from whom the new sound poetry and procedural lyric have much to learn.

Notes

[i]Walt Whitman, *Leaves of Grass*, Ed. Schulley Bradley and Harold W. Blodgett (New York: Norton Critical Edition, 1973), p. 116.

[ii]Frank O'Hara, *Collected Poems*, Ed. Donald Allen (Berkeley, University of California Press, 1995), p. 255.

Marge Piercy

TROUBLE BLOOMING WITH THE DAFFODILS

There's something about the way spring
pulls seeds out of the ground into green
fountains of leaves that makes me want
nothing in particular, just a vague

sense that there should be more.
When I was younger that drew me
into trouble, into beds of rocks
and needles, into webs of knotted

hair in which I almost strangled.
The young dream in blood. Now
I just write a poem. Getting old isn't
as unhealthy as you might think.

Nick Rinaldi

REMEMBERING ROSE

> "I longed to embrace my dead mother's ghost;
> three times I tried to clasp her image, and three
> times it slipped through my hands, like a shadow..."
> –The Odyssey, XI

She went from store to store
in a row of stores along the avenue,
buying knitting yarn, and yards of
cotton and wool. I tagged along,
sucking on penny candy. We passed
the public library and a barbershop,
a savings bank, a bakery, the angled steel girders
of the el along New Utrecht
where the BMT trains wrenched and groaned.

She doesn't have to do that anymore—
sew dresses, or wash the dishes,
the clothes. In those days it wasn't automatic,
she did it all by hand. She doesn't have to
take the BMT to 34th Street, where she
picked up piecework
to do at home. Mostly it was ornaments
for ladies' shoes: long hours by the kitchen window,
getting the bright chrome beads
stitched onto cardboard discs that
someone else would staple
onto glossy pumps, for sale
in bargain basements. She doesn't have to do that
anymore. Defrost the refrigerator,
wax the floor. I was five years old. A butcher cutting meat
winked at her and made a pass.
"Don't be fresh," she answered, blood rising.
The butcher grinned,

and went on carving. Looking back
at the old snapshots, I'm still amazed
how radiant she was. This one: sitting
on a rock by a pond, in a bathing suit,
before she married, bare feet
stirring the water, loose hair
flowing to her waist. Her sexy teenage smile.
And this, the wedding portrait: high cheekbones
and dreamy, pensive eyes,
as if she saw ahead through the slanting, threadbare years
to this off-balance moment when she is
remembered the way garden roses are remembered
long after their season has turned.

The library is still there
and the five-and-ten where I bought marbles
and model planes. Teenagers hang out
on the corners, in leather, smoking pot.
Cops cruise the neighborhood,
two in a car. The trains still run
on the high, rusty el, and somehow she belongs to them,
as she belongs to the small stores
strung out along the avenue: awnings and cracked sidewalks,
smell of warm bread from the bakery, noise of traffic,
and the big glass storefront windows that
caught her reflection and
held it briefly, as she went by.

Pat Schneider

LOVE SONG FOR SISTER AGE

After a long illness
Walk slow
The nowhere that you have

To go

There is a silence after pain
That hurry fills–
A raucous intervention

Pain has taught the rhythm
Of her dance
And when her music's done
There is a silence won
That beatitude can fill

But will

Only if you listen and walk slow
The nowhere that you have
To go

Vivian Shipley

THE STINKING ROSE

I must admit it's the oxymoron of garlic's folk name
in ancient Rome that woos me, not the history.
Rubbed on bodies by legionnaires to ward off colds,
native to the Caucasus, worshipped by Egyptians,

bulbous cloves were shields for the evil eye, thwarted
devourers of blood- vampire, bacteria or mosquito.
In 1652, Nicholas Culpeper recorded garlic healing
bites of mad dogs, ridding children of worms, curing

the plagues, earaches and abscesses. What a choice:
halitosis or teeth marks on my neck. I suppose it
depends on the situation. When Satan stepped out
of the Garden of Eden after the fall of man, garlic

sprang up from the spot where he planted his left foot
and onion from under his right foot. Surely, Satan
did not worry about his breath and would have been
a match for Dracula any day. Garlic's raw sting

sweetens with heat and might have cleansed acid
of the apple on Adam's tongue or could it have been
the aphrodisiac quickening his thighs? Hard to figure
out as original sin, truth does not always announce

itself, can be waiting like garlic in ditches or trenches
by the side of the road. Questions about good and evil
are as difficult to answer as it is to remove parchment
that separates knife from clove. Why garlic can even

surprise a poet who's used to lifting the veil, laying bare
the inside; Percy Shelley wrote from Italy to a friend,
What do you think? Young women of rank eat—you will
never guess what—*garlick!* Shelley did know that sucked

dry of juice, of flavor, of emotion, poems are like prunes,
predictable. With garlic you never know—too little water
when it's growing can invite disaster, too much rain when
the garlic is mature will ruin the crop. If a farmer has

a poet's soul, she stays on an existential edge, will bend
into a hairpin to straighten untidy piles of garlic, because
like muddled lines, stems labeled scapes get tangled.
Fleeting as inspiration can be, garlic lasts six months,

will dry out to papery dust, its inside becomes hollow
or even moldy. Thinking of doing a first draft while
planting garlic, I stick cloves in a furrow, don't worry
if they are sitting straight-posture perfect, they will

right themselves. Soft-neck Asian, Turban Chengdu,
California Early, or Russian Red, all I know for sure
is that since I've upped my garlic intake, I haven't been
pestered by vampires—or for that matter, anyone else.

Betsy Sholl

STARRY NIGHT

Once I had several dreams in the same week, each telling me I could let the worst happen and step away, alive in a field so bright no way to paint it but with thick globs and swirls of green. So, let others build their barricades against disappointment and death, against what ruin will or will not strike with its one blue bolt to the heart, its crows crowding in, stifling the sky, iron everywhere. Let the gold finches disappear into this pair of young maples, deep into the leaves. When they fall, come autumn, we'll find two thimble-sized nests, thistle down and milkweed tied to a crook with spider thread. Who needs straight lines? All those theories about how Van Gogh got to his whirling stars—absinthe, cataracts, madness. But can't someone let the facts go and just paint how it feels under a star-splattered sky, light splotched, night kissed, and for once no longer separate, not locked out? A moment irony would never allow, and bitterness would surely miss, with its grim resentment that counts every slight. But how my grandfather's garden flourished! Grandfather of shame, of the stiff raised cane, harsh word, stony silence the earth kept trying to woo. From the roof of our chicken coop my sisters and I watched the last finches twitter and dip toward their roosts, as the cedar's lace grew dark, and the night sky got ready to bloom. Beneath us, grapes nestled in their leaves, pumpkins grew fat as orange hassocks, and potatoes slowly inched out their eye beams like stars hidden in the dirt— or what could have been stars if allowed to shine.

Justin St. Germain

220 Kingston St., June 1, 2009

The boxes are packed, stacked, waiting to be hauled to a storage unit by the highway. My roommates and I are moving out. In two weeks we'll give this apartment back how we got it: cobwebbed corners, carpet stained, half the light bulbs dead, dusty. The dust, like most domestic dust, came from bodies, ours and the bodies of the people who were here before us, the people who've passed through.

This apartment still gets mail for a lot of them: bills, literary magazines, collection notices, sometimes cards. I know some of the former residents, recognize the names of others. Most of them are writers. The last renter left us some bookshelves, and when we moved them across the room, we found a picture of another former resident taped to the side. After we moved in, the guy in the picture asked me to take photos out the living room window to use in his book, which begins in this living room. I sometimes like to think of this apartment as a place people pass through on their way to somewhere better. But I think that about everywhere I live.

The last place I lived for this long was a house I shared with my brother in Tucson when we were in college, a run-down bungalow on East Lee St. I moved into during the summer of 2000. Soon after that, our mother was murdered, and soon after that I moved out. In the eight years since, I've had a dozen addresses. I don't know why I've moved so much; I've only lived in two cities during that time. Maybe I inherited my mother's restlessness: when I was a kid, we lived in so many houses—easily more than twenty—that I can't even remember some of them. She'd buy a house, move us in, and put it on the market the next day. We'd move into her boyfriends' houses and then out again a few months later. She married five times and I lived in houses with stepdads and stepsiblings, people I liked or disliked but in either case had to tolerate. In that sense, I've had roommates my entire life, people passing through.

A few months ago I came home to find a group of people sitting at our kitchen table drinking wine. They were friends of my roommate's, the poet. He introduced us. One was a thin, tallish man with a shaved head. He reminded me a little bit of Michael Stipe. His name was Craig. He stayed on our couch for a couple of nights, but I wasn't home much and neither was he, so we didn't really get to talk. My impression of him was mostly his bags and clothes lying on the floor of this living room. I gleaned that he was a professor and a poet, had a girlfriend and a son, and that he was on his way to Japan to do research for a book. The book was about volcanoes.

A month later he went missing on an island in Japan. I followed the search for him on the internet, checking each day for good news that never came. At somebody's request, I sent a letter to my senator. Eventually his trail was followed to the edge of a cliff. He'd been missing for weeks. His body was never found.

I didn't know Craig. The grief of his loss does not belong to me, and I make no claim to it. But since he left, I've often thought of him, sleeping on that dingy couch we inherited. I've thought of how awful it must be for his loved ones. I've wondered what it means that he left this apartment—like so many others before him have left, and like we will soon leave—and went to Japan. Whether it means anything.

The last person to report seeing my mother alive was a neighbor she hardly knew. The neighbor saw my mother's truck driving down a dirt road in rural Arizona. It was late morning, around ten. The coroner later estimated that she died a few hours later. I never spoke to the neighbor afterward; I read her statement in a police report. I'm leaving this apartment and going to Arizona to do research for a book. The book is about my mother. I could find the neighbor and talk to her, ask her if she ever wonders what it means that she saw my mother just before she died. I could ask her whether it means anything. Does she see trucks pass on that road and think of her, like I've thought of Craig these last few months while walking through this living room? Or has she moved since then, and forgotten?

Marilyn L. Taylor

THE TROUBLE WITH AUTOBIOGRAPHY

Although we may try
to stick to the truth,
our life stories
are mostly fiction.

To call them the truth
without embellishment
will either be fiction
or wishful thinking;

Any embellishment
will conjure stories
of wishful thinking
artfully re-arranged—

stories conjured
straight out of bedlam
but re-arranged
into tidy plots.

Is bedlam still bedlam
when told as a tale?
Will our tidy plots
twist the narrative

into tall tales?
Yet we can't help
but twist our narratives
to suit ourselves,

can't help it
that our "life stories"
tell a different story—
although we may try.

Steven Teref

CONFESSION OF AN ORTHODOX PRIEST

St. Sava Temple: God's marble finger. Under the nail: the fungal underbelly of purgatory. The bones of St. Sava burn in concrete flames. Balkan shadows end in Cyrillic pools of toenail polish. The anonymous live with prayer scars for all the kneeling nights unanswered. I speak umber silence in a city ruled by a modern coconut deity and its discontents with creased sneakers, remainder books, fragrance-free masks. Cast-asides force the view of emaciated corpses rotting in tree branches, draped like drying bed sheets in the heat. The riverside villages along the Drina: bones strewn along iron mud banks. From pear branches, brandy bottles dangle like diamond earrings.

Steven Teref

TO THE HOLY GHOST

You fashion faith from void. The hatred without within awaiting virgin
birth. I can't sing. My broken throat rasps. You embody the history of
prayer and forgiveness, you carny catalytic converter. How else could
Christ be moved to transmogrify me from an auto mechanic's sponge
into a gold chalice cradling holy blood? I'm afraid of the distance.
Either you create God or you leave town.

Jeanie Thompson

HELEN KELLER WITH THE MARTHA GRAHAM DANCE COMPANY
—New York, 1954

To move on feet like these requires a different sight.
The floor shook. With a new rhythm of their footfalls
and the lift of their toes, I knew their vibrant light.

The small one, their master whose very body spelled breath,
guided me to a young man, a gnarled foot I held.
To move on feet like these requires a different sight.

His toes pointing the urge to be up and up, that height,
the subtle heat of their bodies, their movement called.
With the lift of their toes, I knew their vibrant light.

When she pulled me into them, a current ran, spear-like,
tightening, as if my whole body were a palm.
To move on feet like these requires a different sight.

My sturdy shoes on that elastic floor knew joy uplifted
and she – rod-straight and lithe, her body hard, a calm
praise for the lift of their toes, that vibrant life–

She sheared around us–a star, a comet whose bright
corona poured forth joy's spoken filaments. All
to move on feet like these–a different sight!
To know the lift of their toes, I moved in their vibrant light.

JIM

A woman wearing glasses brings me shoes. She offers them at arm's length. "If they're not your size," she says, "I can take them back."

She looks down, and I follow her gaze to the hole in my left shoe where a toe protrudes like a ghostly toadstool from the shadows of worn leather. Beneath the shoe, snow patinas the city sidewalk. It doesn't snow often in Alabama, but it is snowing now.

"Aren't you cold?" she asks. "Your coat has a hole in it. My father had a coat that might fit." Her face goes still.

"Is your father dead?"

"I—"

The words she needs to say lodge between mind and heart. I see them through the transparency of her heavy coat and skin, stuck on the bony thorns of her spine.

She pulls her red wool coat tighter. "That's not what I meant to imply."

I haven't moved to take the shoes, so she sets them on the sidewalk, perfectly aligned, the right nestling into the left, curving toward one another with the knowing that they belong together. She steps back. "I meant to say that I noticed you standing on this corner the past few days and saw that you needed shoes."

She is breathless. She walked to my corner as though wading against an undertow. Now she seeks shelter from her deed, a retreat. "So I bought you a pair," she says. "That's all."

"Thank you." I scratch at the thick bramble of my frosted beard.

"You're welcome," she replies crisply, back in her fortress.

When she is gone, I pick up the shoes and put them in the bushes.

§

"Did the shoes not fit?"

She is back. The woman with the glasses.

"I don't know."

She stiffens. Wind slaps a tendril of hair against her cheek. "You didn't even try them on, did you?"

When I don't reply, she makes an indignant sound and stomps away, though the snow eats the clap of her boot heels.

§

Two days later, I am deep into my prayers. I feel her at my elbow, but I can't look at her. I haven't finished. The words have to flow all on one breath. If they are not a perfect offering three times in succession, I cannot move on. Across the street there is a bench beside a raised flowerbed planted with purple cabbage. I've been four days here, and I want to cross the street and sit on the bench where I can watch the pigeons and the purple cabbage between prayer times.

"I'm sorry I got huffy over the shoes," the woman says.

Distracted, I miss a word of the prayer. My fists clench. Now, I must stay on this corner another three days. The human part of me wants to shout and shake her.

The divine part turns to her. "You are forgiven."

She blinks. "What did you do with the shoes?"

"I hid them."

She is still for a moment, but I am not going to try to return to the prayers. I must have silence, and she is not going to be silent. Above us, the traffic light changes to yellow. Prayers must fit into the time between their cycling. How would I know when to start and finish without them?

"You don't have to hide the shoes," she says, her voice edged with desperate reasonableness. "If you wear them out, I can bring you another pair."

"You are a good person," I say.

She takes a tiny breath, as if it is all she is allowed.

A car passes close to the curb, splashing dirty snow-mush on us. She jumps back, pushing the glasses back onto the bridge of her nose. It is a well-made nose. Freckles pebble it, though she has tried to cover them with makeup.

"May I ask you something?" she says.

I wait.

"Why are you here?"

I lift my face to catch the whisper of flakes that have begun to fall. "Because I'm not perfect."

"I mean, why do you stand on the corner every day like this?" She frowns. "What do you eat? Can't you go to a shelter or . . . something?"

"You are alone in the dark." I say.

She stares at me and takes a step back. "Christ, I just wanted to give you some shoes. Why do you say something like that?"

I wait.

"You don't know me," she says. "You don't know anything about me."

She is gone again, and I return to my prayers.

§

I notice her the next two mornings. She passes on the other side of the street at a steady, measured clip, her face turned away.

The prayers are difficult today. A man drops a hot biscuit in my coat pocket. It is wrapped tight in paper, so I will eat it later. With a twist of his head, a young boy, attached to his mother's arm, stares at me.

"He stinks, Mom."

His mother drags him away.

That evening the woman appears again, a cop at her side, but it's all right because I've just finished. The prayers went perfectly, even the hard ones wisped from my lips into the ether without a falter, perfect pearls formed in the hard belly of my imperfections.

"This is the man," she says to the policeman.

He smiles. "Hello, Jim."

"Good evening, officer. How is your little girl?"

"Growing," he says. "I got a picture here somewhere." He pulls out a wallet and produces a photo.

I nod, glad my prayers have been heard and she, at least, is safe.

The woman watches with her mouth slightly parted. "You know him?" she asks the officer.

"Sure," he says. "Jim's a regular."

"But I've never seen him before last week and I walk this way to work."

The officer shrugs. "He makes his way around the whole city. It takes a while and the odds of seeing him aren't that big."

"But can't you do something?" she protests.

"You mean about him standing on a corner?" He ain't hurting anybody. What's the charge?"

"There's got to be something."

The officer shrugs. "Jim doesn't drink or do drugs; never asks anybody for anything. People just bring him things. He puts most of the stuff in the bushes, and other homeless people get it. They know to look around near wherever he's standing."

She pulls at her coat in offense. The red collar is stark against her pale skin, though the cold has pinked her cheeks and nose. "But he's a vagrant," she says.

"No law against that ma'am. It was struck down in '63 during the Civil Rights stuff. I'm just a police officer. All I can do is enforce laws, and Jim's not breaking any of them."

Her foot taps the ground, as if it wanted to stamp, but was too well mannered.

"Look at him, officer. He stands on that corner all day in the freezing cold mumbling to himself. You know he needs help."

"Are you kin to him?"

Her eyes dart sideways. "No, I'm not. I didn't even know his name."

"Well, if you were, you could try to sign a petition on him, but you'd still have to prove he's a danger to himself or others, otherwise nobody can touch him against his will."

My eyes close and though my feet remain standing on the sidewalk, I am back in the state hospital:

I shuffle to the glass partition that separates us from the night attendants, pressing my ear against the thick pane to hear the voice inside. The TV is turned so I can't see it, but I hear—an earthquake in Haiti has killed thousands of people; a school in India collapsed in a flood; a child in Illinois found locked in a basement, starved, beaten, and sexually abused. The endless horrors are reported daily, because I am trapped in here and can't say the prayers. I slap my palm against the thick glass.

The female attendant looks up through her layered bangs. The dark roots, bleeding into the blonde ice, are an inch long now, how I measure time. "Go away, Jim."

I slap the glass again. "I can't say my prayers."

She ignores me.

"I can't [slap] say [slap] them."

Annoyed, she finally looks up. "Do you need a shot, Jim?"

"No."

"What do you want?"

"I have to say my prayers, and I can't say them."

"Why not?" Her gaze drifts back to the picture on the TV that is out of my line of sight. I can see in her eyes the reflection of an overturned bus and glimpses of twisted, burned limbs.

My cheek presses against the glass wall. "The pills take away my prayers," I whisper. "They take away my prayers ... and the world is lost."

§

The voice of the woman with the glasses catapults me back to the corner where I stand between her and the policeman.

"How can you say he's not a danger to himself out here in the cold like this? What does he eat? Where does he sleep?"

"Ma'am, there's simply not enough room in the institutions if judges ruled everyone who was homeless or nuts needed to be picked up. I know you mean well, but Jim doesn't want any help. Why don't you go volunteer at the Firehouse Shelter? They always need people."

"I can't believe this," she says. "What kind of world is this?"

It is my question too.

He regards her. "There's worse cases than Jim all over this city. Most people don't see 'cause they don't want to look."

§

It is evening. I face the west, which makes it difficult to see the traffic light. A man shuffles up to me. "Hey, Jim. I got the shoes you put out, and I was late to the Shelter, so I ate the sandwich too."

I nod, my eyes on the signal light.

He puts a hand on my shoulder, and I flinch away.

"Sorry man, I forgot you don't like to be touched."

The light turns red and I begin.

§

In dawn light that furs the city without warmth, I move with slow, reverent steps across the street. Wind flaps my coat. The light has changed for me, a deep blood red. On the other side, I face the road to say the first morning prayer. Then I go to the bench and sit.

Later, I see her walking up the sidewalk across the street. Her stride is not so confident, so sure of where she is going. Her head lifts in surprise when she realizes I am no longer on that corner, and she looks around before catching sight of me on the bench.

Without waiting for the light, she tap-taps across. "I'm glad you're still here," she says. "I thought for a moment you were gone."

I wait.

"You don't care do you?"

"I'm waiting," I say.

Wind tangles her hair and she tries to tame it behind her ears. "For what?"

I don't answer.

She begins to pace in front of the bench. "I don't know why I came over here."

Snowflakes fall into her hair and glimmer in the streetlight which is still on though, fooled by the cover of clouds.

Now she is looking up at the traffic light, which is yellow. Her breath clouds briefly. "I wanted to tell you—"

She hesitates, but I nod. She is dragging up those words that have been caught on the thorns of her pain, but then she tucks her gloved hands under her armpits and says instead, "I don't know why you want to live like this. It's not right for you to be out here. There's something terribly wrong that you are."

She takes a deep breath, exhaling another tiny cloud. "I know you're not responsible. You're mixed up and doing your best somehow."

These are not the words that must be said, so I keep waiting.

She sits beside me on the bench, not too close, and takes another breath, reaching through the hurt for the words she must say.

"I wanted to help you . . . because my father died a month ago. It was a long illness, and I didn't—" She looks away and then back at me again, determined. Tears jewel her eyes. "I wasn't the daughter I should have been."

These are the words.

I turn to her, meeting her eyes. "You are forgiven."

She stares at me for a long time and then takes my hand in both of hers. I don't jerk away from her. I let it rest between the soft leather gloves, looking back at the traffic light.

When she leaves, I shuffle to the corner to say the prayers.

Diane Wakoski

REAR VIEW

Because I am held in the blue gloves
of my Honda, and I want to back out,
I must swivel around to view my driveway.
Someone is standing beside it,
but with the head of a crocodile
instead of a face.
Shocked,
I check the rearview mirror.
But now the figure is obscured by
a flood of light.
One more glance backward,
turning my head to check clearance.
And it is you, Steelman!
Your old self.
Now a peek in the rearview.
Confirmed. No alligator in my driveway.

You wave, as I back out, motor away.
That figure, perhaps Anubis from Egyptian stories,
whose jackal head always seemed more crocodilian
than doggish to me,
might be out there at the end
of my driveway, taking my husband's body
for a flash, just as I look backward.
My rear view looks
are haunted by shape shifters.
Thank the gods I seldom have to look back
any more and soon will stop driving.
Death then will be my chauffeur.
I've already seen him driving me down Easy Street,
and have mentioned the fragility of my heart
in its locked suitcase in the trunk,
waiting to be weighed like a feather.

At Video To Go, I look for a film
about gambling, about trickery, something that,
like "Shade" which I've already seen,
will educate me in the ways of life and death. I think of
checking out a DVD about Derrida,
then the BBC documentary "Following In The Footsteps
of Alexander the Great," and even one
about bird migration. Inadvertently, I see a box with
a crocodile on the cover, and it says
"Nothing In The Box," by Ron Padgett*.
Shock/ It is a morning of shocks.
Earlier, I saw a "Def Poetry Jam" disc, but didn't think
even this good store was stocking literary poets like Padgett
on DVD. And what was with
the crocodile?
Maybe it's one of those DVDs that you watch
and then die or have some
supernatural experience? Decide
it's too weird to check out. Find myself
a copy of a safe film:
"Spellbound".

I have watched Hitchcock's "Rear Window"
a few times, but never got into it.
I myself live in a house with virtually no curtains
on any of the windows. Never
think of looking in other people's windows,
except when driving at night, and they look
like old *Saturday Evening Post* covers.
Never imagine anyone looking in mine,
though a former student in our university town said
she used to walk by our house all the time,
just to see all the filled bookshelves lining our walls
in both up and downstairs windows.

I can't imagine seeing, from these naked
windows a rifle pointing anywhere, or even though
this house is filled with cameras, I don't

imagine a Hasselblad pointing
in or out of any window. Though
in my own camera eye,
I often see Saturn's rings.
And if I turn away from my computer and Steelman
is coming into the room, I know
in this safe and protected house,
I would not, would not, even see
the man with crocodile head and teeth.
                Like Orpheus,
                        I have made my long black journey.
Unlike Orpheus, I know
I am leaving behind nothing
I was meant to take.

*Ron Padgett's famous poem is *Nothing In That Drawer*

Margaret Watson

SCION

Hours **S**pent in front

of a mirror make a picture

a gaze wit**H**in two perfect

eyes are wasted, never

time le**A**ds summer on to

winter, too hideous with frost

leaves **K**een spent and beauty,

bareness **E**verywhere, no where

no summer'**S** left all that's left,

a liquid **P**risoner of glass

beauty evaporat**E**s like its metaphor

no remember**A**nce what it was

in a mirro**R** meeting, show,

short but sw**E**et

Isabelle Whitman

BRUISES LIKE FLOWERS

I am so over rot.
I am tired of the filth, the shit, the scum,
the bloated corpse.
I am weary of the overwrought:
the weeping mothers and fresh orphans.

Another body. Another fatal wound. Another victim, and another and
another and another skull split sideways, another torso full of holes, so many
holes, so many guts, so much stuff comes out of strung out girls, or flung out
males, their bodies slumped in parking lots, the whole damn lot of them are
useless fucking scum senseless wastes of skin and breath and shit–

I wanted poetry.
I wanted them splayed artfully
at river's edge, hair fanning out
in waves on the Mississippi,
bruises like flowers on their fragile throats.
I wanted to be hero of the dead girls,
cigarette stuck firm in stern set mouth,
a strong and silent modern Marlowe,
the Marlboro Man of Orleans Parish.
I wanted to fuck the ones who lived
after I put away the men who killed their sisters,

but I got dead girls
with ugly boyfriends, broken teeth
and neck tattoos of misspelled names,
missing kids and dead boys too young to buy beer
and too old to put aside their streetworn pride.
These bruises don't bloom,
but spread instead
like sticky stains on dirty carpets.
Blood spatters, then crusts,

and there is no poetry in scabs.
I am no hero here,
just one man standing
ankle deep in rot.

Carey Scott Wilkerson

ARIADNE IN EXILE

Cast

ARIADNE: Princess of Crete and former lover of Theseus, who has abandoned HER on the Island of Naxos.

DIONYSUS: The god of wine, sex, and ecstatic rituals.

CHORUS

SCENE ONE
(ARIADNE is seated silently onstage)
(CHORUS enters and to the audience)

CHORUS
Witness this story of classic, not to say, classical heartbreak.
Observe here young Ariadne, Princess of Crete,
daughter of dread Minos, keeper of royal secrets.
She possesses an acute sense of history, a map of the sky,
a library card, and an MFA in radical self-narration.
She was mastermind of Theseus's mission to slay the Minotaur
and escape from the Labyrinth, guided by a clue of yarn,
a trail leading him back to daylight and back to her arms.
Dreaming of a future in Athens wearing Stuart Weitzman shoes
and a Hermes handbag, she sailed with Theseus toward a new life.
But Theseus had certain plans of his own.
Far from Athens and far from her home,
Ariadne is abandoned on Naxos alone.

ARIADNE (to the audience)

It's not as though I haven't seen first-hand the ruinous consequence of choosing the wrong partner in life. My mother Pasiphaë certainly did not believe in my father's imperious style or his absurd war with the

Athenians. For his part, he cannot have been happy about my mother's affair with that magical Taurus. You know, the result of which was the Minotaur, half man, half bull. When your wife has sex an animal and gives birth to a creature that will doom an entire generation of children, becoming part of a mythic metaphor for troubled families and primordial terror, it's hard to recover from that. Dinners grow suddenly quiet. Family reunions are, in a word, confusing. When the Minotaur was a still young, he seemed somehow out-of-place grazing at the kid's table. But he had his head on straight, more or less, about his role in the world. He knew he didn't belong anywhere. He belonged nowhere. And would always be the monstrous Other.

CHORUS

The identity of "monstrous Other"
is essentially a question of semantics.
The Minotaur was a creature divided
against itself, split from within.
Is this not true of us all?

ARIADNE

My mother's transgressive move with the magic bull, a gift to my father from Poseidon, means The Minotaur was my half-brother. This takes the non-traditional family structure to an exotic new level. I still don't know how to feel about that or if I should feel any way at all. My father obsessed over rules his entire life. But looking back, there seem to have been so few rules. My mother clearly had weak boundaries. I suppose the same could be said of me. I, too, wanted something odd, a foreign prince, my father's sworn enemy, an unattainable mythic hero with his reputation and his big sword.

CHORUS

You wanted what you could not have.
Is it really so strange?
This is a familiar pattern in many lives.

ARIADNE

Well, I make a distinction between that which "one cannot have" and that which "one should not have." Without putting too fine a point on it,

Theseus was in the second category. By any measure, he was forbidden. And while it's true that I did want him, what's important is that I had him. I got him. He was mine. True, my mother warned about men like him. But sensing her jealousy, I reminded her that at least my man was, you know, a man and not the star attraction in a petting zoo. Or first place in his weight class at the state fair.

CHORUS

But Theseus, for all his wonders,
did not turn out to be the answer you had hoped for.
He has plundered your heart and left you here
alone with Dionysus, god of sex…and some other things.

(CHORUS exits.)

(DIONYSUS enters)

DIONYSUS

Ariadne, my sweet, my splendid flower, my lucent honey ball! I have come once again to hold you in passion's thrall. Do you not delight in my scintillating repartée? Do you not search the moonlight for my penetrating eyes?

ARIADNE

Well, yes, every night with you is, by definition, Dionysian. But it's not the good company that keeps my attention. And it's not the penetrating eyes.

DIONYSUS

Is it the way we sat up late?

ARIADNE

That's part of it.

DIONYSUS

Is the way I always want to be with you.

ARIADNE

That's nice, too.

DIONYSUS

I remember your birthday. And our anniversary. I know your favorite constellations.

ARIADNE

Also very nice.

DIONYSUS (weary of the charade)

You know, I really am trying hard here.

ARIADNE

I can see that, but…

DIONYSUS

I thought we had worked all this out.

ARIADNE

Let's not assign blame. Counseling only goes so far.

DIONYSUS

What's your point?

ARIADNE

I'm an attractive, intelligent woman. And you are the god of sex. I think she was expecting that we'd have better stories.

DIONYSUS

I'm telling my therapist I no longer believe in counseling. Better stories? Are you serious?

ARIADNE

Yes. Do you want to know how I know she was expecting better stories? Okay, I'll tell you: because I was expecting better stories.

(DIONYSUS exits, grim and dejected.)

(ARIADNE addresses the audience.)

I know what you're thinking: what an ungrateful, entitled little princess or perhaps a variation on that basic idea? I confess that discovering I had been left on Naxos with Dionysus was exciting at first. And I probably thought a life with him would mean some kind of final deliverance from Theseus's betrayal. And if I'm really honest, I suppose it felt like the perfect revenge. I would spend the rest of my life in bed with the deity of cosmic passion, doing things on a cosmic scale. Sure, there was plenty of that. But the cruel irony is that after Theseus, I wanted something less complicated. And wouldn't you know it, the moment I arrived, the god of sex himself decided he wanted something more transcendent!

(CHORUS enters.)

CHORUS

You have issues with bad timing.
Or perhaps it is a matter of fate.
You were unhappy on Crete.
And then your hero took you away.
But he was a disappointment.
Then you discovered another lover on Naxos
who also failed to deliver on the dreams
you have held so close to your heart.
Perhaps you are fated to a life in art.

ARIADNE

Please no! Not that!

END SCENE

SCENE TWO

Years have passed.
ARIADNE, wearing glasses, sits alone on the beach of Naxos.
In the distance, a ship is approaching.

(SHE addresses the audience.)

ARIADNE

By the time I was ready to admit I had been a fool, Dionysus was gone. I guess being the god of sex is not quite the same as being a sex god. Those are purely fiction, it seems. But he did leave behind the house, the vineyard, a respectable collection of books. Too much poetry and drama for my taste, but still enough to keep me busy forever. Or until that ship, which has just appeared at the horizon, finally gets here. It moves so slowly. Watching it reminds me of that same scene when I was a girl, waiting for some adventure to arrive from a distant shore, to take me away to a life of romance and fantasy. It turns out that the waiting was itself the fantasy. Although I had no way of knowing it, I had become the proto-Romantic figure of my own irrational storyline. And I still am. I have to tell my own story since the Chorus has retired. They have remained here to help with the harvest and to catalog books. They are all insane and probably only projections of my imagination, but these days it's the closest thing I have to a family. And it's the best family I ever had.

(SHE searches the horizon.)

This is a great lesson of endurance, and metaphysics. Whatever we're waiting for seems to approach only when we're looking away. Looking back on what we've lost is strangely the opposite. It seems always with us. What we have lost is always with us. We cannot lose it. We cannot escape it. I guess the Aristotelian view of quantum physics would be that it is somehow an extension of philosophy itself. My memory of a future in which Theseus would kiss me at the Labyrinth gate is as present to me--a woman-of-a-certain-age--as the hope of a touch, that would dispel that past, was suddenly manifest in a Dionysian swirl.

(SHE searches the horizon.)

It's stating the obvious to say that we are all torn between desire and destiny just as surely as I was torn between two phantoms of my own inner duplicity. I can speak this way without feeling self-conscious because I'm old enough to see the truth in it. You don't have to believe me.

(SHE searches the horizon. CHORUS enters.)

I think I know something now that I didn't know before about the Minotaur and what it means to be your own ontological shadow: yourself and perhaps also another.

(SHE searches the horizon.)

But don't take my word for it.

CHORUS

Observe here Ariadne,
Princess of Crete, Queen of Naxos,
gazing expectantly across the dazzling Aegean Sea.

END

Christian Wiman

EVEN THE DEMON

It takes a real cow
to bite beyond
the prickly pear's
sharp spokes.

It takes a brain
of stone
or canny man
to coax

from thorn and husk
sustaining fruit.
It takes hunger,
it takes thirst

to taste

Christian Wiman

HERE VISIBLE

Here visible
distance

is so much
a part

of things
things

acquire a kind
of space:

I reach
right through

the raking
tooth

that for so long
I've longed

to show you.
I touch

eternity
in your face.

Amy Wright

SNO-CONE CANDELABRA

Green

I helped my father work the carnival. He was a Lion and the club sponsored the much-anticipated summer event that came to town every July. His tent was the muffin tin game. On a waist-high table, painted tins were laid, one hole in four dozen awaiting an airily imprecise wiffle ball to crown its white ring. When a winner would sink, a siren would wail and rise, threatening to erupt from the candy-corn-yellow-lit tent.

"When did you get those?" my soon-to-be high school boyfriend asked, looking at my chest. Daniel was a wrestler who'd been eying me awhile, coming up with illogical excuses to carry me up the stairs damsel-style after lunch. He called sometimes, but we hadn't seen each other all summer. Walking around the carnival that night, his two-year plan was starting to come together.

He thought me bold because the first time I met him—an eighth grader still new to high school—I walked alone up to his locker, a junior's, where he was standing with another boy. I told him my best friend, Andie, thought he was cute. It was true, but it wasn't my truth.

Andie thought me bold too from the way I made her acquaintance. We were eleven and sitting on the sidelines of a softball game. "I don't like math either," I said to her, "but it's not like batting is even useful for anything else." My comment seemed a natural icebreaker for two girls whose biceps were not cut out for these practices, but years later she told me it surprised her I had spoken to her since we were strangers. We were in sixth grade! We were strangers to ourselves. Perhaps because I transferred schools in fourth grade, I had a leg up on small town kids making introductions. By then, I had already met and lost the one I loved. Joseph Music. He had the greenest eyes, the leanest jaw, the brownest arms—Joseph From-Where-The-Music-Comes.

Daniel and I rode the Ferris wheel and looked out at the fields beyond town. He prided himself on being a gentleman, so he didn't kiss me until much later, standing in a dark garage at the Corey's house while a party ground like a roller coaster behind us. He opened a side door and slipped us out the back while my stomach cranked into my chest. Ushering me onto a step to equal our heights, he put his hand to my cheek, his mouth feeling for the switch of my tongue that would start the siren's climb.

Orange

I met a lot of deer while running trails—mule deer in the Colorado Flatirons, shy white-tails in Virginia. On my best runs my legs unfurl and I am one, dashing between trees and across fallen limbs. One afternoon a doe in sweet clover stopped grazing and stood watching me. I paused my stride and looked back at her. She was made of fire. We watched it in each other. Blazes flickered behind the gates of our eyes. Two Liberty Bells turned toward each other to crack. Then she bolted, not knowing whether such a thing was safe.

Neither my father nor my grandfather hunted, though someone had given Grandad a blaze orange hat with flaps he wore when he was out mending fence or feeding calves. Assuming that shock of color was to protect him during firearms season, I asked Mom if we shouldn't also wear something to distinguish ourselves. Deer often grazed the fields surrounding our house, nibbling apple trees in our yard, and come November, I imagined my umber corduroys looked from two hundred yards like fur.

In the summer, I feared being mistaken by our garden fence. To discourage the long-legged creatures from jumping it, my mother had strung cheap scented soaps over each post. When the perfume failed to keep them out, Dad looped the periphery with a string of electricity. The box feeding the current hummed with a constant chirm of power, low as the vibration of a June bug. Buzzing, alive, the stream of wire could flood a body with a charge as comprehensive as lust.

Yellow

There is a tourist attraction in Perth, Australia called Swan Bells. The twelve bells of St. Martin-in-the-Fields are one of the oldest and loudest musical instruments in the world. To hear them in person is to allow yourself to be rung with a pitch that can surface myriad feelings and leave what is known as a 'chiming' memory.

My grandmother collected bells. Schoolhouse bells. Wedding cake bells. Cow bells. Bells made of mother of pearl shells, balsa wood. I didn't know she collected them until my mother displayed the ones she inherited on a pie safe in the dining room. I had thought she collected candy in dishes because she wouldn't let us eat those little rocks of light.

I never heard anyone ring the dinner bell at the end of the gate, but when my mother was young, Granny tolled it to bring Granddad and the boys in from the fields to eat dinner. Or she wouldn't. They would come when he reached a stopping place and the girls, hungry, would wait.

It hung above the fence, which I climbed once to clang, wanting to hear it carry over the hills. The reverberation filled my chest with something like that blossoming force I imagined split the Incredible Hulk's shirt. I got in trouble, though I wasn't sure afterward why I was forbidden to swing its tongue again. On his Case tractor or inside the cab of his old Ford, my grandfather wouldn't have heard the knell, much less come to it. Maybe it just seemed wrong to her for a child to make a plaything of its resounding, welling up and spilling over that iron lip like the deep kisses she never let us catch them giving. It wouldn't dent like that soft metal, gold.

When I pull the shank of a sapphire ring that Daniel gave me from my jewelry box, I remember learning gold's delicacy. The same metal my grandfather wore to the barn—his solid band a perfect circle after decades handling gear shifts and stuck gates—marred under my sixteen year old hand. Had I knocked it against some bleacher, squeezed it into a jar lid, gripped my steering wheel too hard? If gold was this tender, I considered I might need to have my wedding ring cast of bronze or copper, like those change-ringing bells that trumpet the Perth Tower with variable song.

Blue

There was a terrarium in my grandmother's sunlit parlor, steamy with enclosed humidity, another world washed by its own breath. Sitting on her couch was like being inside a snow globe in which rainbows rise and fall instead of flakes. The condensation shimmered from the glass-lined window ledge above—pigeon's blood red, seafoam green, candy apple blue—the shade of my first bike according to a note my mother tucked inside a Christmas tree ornament: *There is something new and candy apple blue waiting in the garage for you.* I ran to the garage and rode around it in circles, snow covering the ground outside, silver jingle bells tied to the laces of my shoes.

Purple

A string of my grandmother's bells hangs from a silk cord in my living room. They sound a brass rain when I open the balcony doors, startling the starlings in the birches into shaving their beards of song. Its chime carries out in concentric circles before the sound swallows itself like water around a diver, and I am left standing as if on a pier onto which leaves fall and are swept into the wind to fall.

My mother has been reluctant to pass her mother's things to me. At ten, I lost an antique opal ring of hers at a campground, the same campground where Daniel would return from his first semester at college to break up with me. My friend's dog Percy avoids a section of the park where he once met a fox. But even if I skirt the camp road to avoid its memories, a tone can conjure the loneliness of feeding quarters into the pinball machine at the camp arcade for hours after Daniel left. An echo of that ricochet catches me off guard in pool halls and preschools, at chirping crosswalks. A crying ambulance recalls those summer weeks I inhabited another life in which I was a carny's gypsy daughter, a dame rescued from the lunchroom railroad crossing, and I thrum seemingly without cause.

I wonder if my father doesn't experience something similar when he hears a helicopter or bandages coming off, a television late at night conjuring air raids.

He was stationed as a medic in Vietnam, before he and my mother married. In a photograph of him taken there, he is standing outside an Army tent, eighteen, skinny and blonde, bare chested in dogtags. It must have been taken in the afterglow of adrenalin because he looks flushed, radiant with distance. Whereas my father sold insurance and married his high school sweetheart and wouldn't eat a hot dog without chili, this man was something else. Someone I could imagine falling in love with for the first time.

He had a box in his closet my mother and I came upon once during spring cleaning. Before I realized what it was, I saw a medal and asked her "Did Dad get a purple heart?" "No, honey, that's for men who are wounded and thank God your father wasn't." "Then why does he have that?" My eleven-year-old self already knew not to ask him too many questions. He volunteered more than he answered about those two years, and he didn't volunteer much.

Closing the lid, she didn't explain the ribbon either, though I assume from its inglorious position in the box it was some lesser medal, though the imprint was made. Was it not heart-coloring to be pulled from home so young to tend men who died, friends who went mad? Standing outside the carnival tent with Daniel, did that picture come to mind? Of a boy becoming a man, whose eyes glinting in the sun could see things he would not have me imagine, which shone with a royal stain.

Red

Now in her sixties, my mother has grown more willing to part with a few of my grandmother's things. She was right to wait. I respect the gravity of these items, which offer in the passing of things the closest I can get to making more memories.

When I ring a bell from India my mother gave me from my grandmother's collection, the air shudders with rings, the way my eyes hovered over the muffin tins while balls sailed through the air. Full of holes and light, they floated wishful and watched over the roped table where tins gaped like mouths. At last, one ball would bounce, bumped, to settle into a star position. The thrower would shout and the tent fatten with siren swell, while my father or one of his fellow Lions would tear down a bear from the rafters, its felt tongue flapping in its mouth. All other players would stop and behold this triumph, which was also great advertisement, as clusters amassed around the lucky couple.

And it was luck. My father assured me of the impossibility of aiming a wiffle ball from ten feet back through a draft of night air. I imagine he had been such a fool at one time, as those strapping showoffs peeling bills from their wallets. Perhaps going to war and making it back alive showed him the odds of such great fortune as meeting my mother, for the lesson carried him over forty years of marriage with the sureness of aim.

After the siren peaked, the carnival tent would drop into relative silence. The short interim hung heavy as the clapper of an iron bell, urgent to be heard, before some voice pealed through the clearing blood-bright as a branch unzipped by a cardinal.

After that intoxicating week of sno-cone highs and stuffed-puppy-winning romance, the carnival packed up its tents and left town. The Lions stayed late on the last night to stack muffin tins and bull's eye targets, lazy river prizes. My Dad went back with the others on Sunday afternoon to fold up the stage. I didn't help with cleanup, so my memory of the carnival is of being lit up, my world as big as it had ever been and then just as gone—carousel, ticket booths, house of mirrors, rides. Not even the litter of cola cups blew around. It was a field behind the college, nothing more than that. Quiet. A seasonal loss.

Reaching After Fact

DICK ALLEN is the current Connecticut Poet Laureate (2010-2015), following John Hollander. Allen's eighth poetry collection, *This Shadowy Place* (St. Augustine's Press, 2014), won the 2013 New Criterion Poetry Prize. His three previous books are *Present Vanishing: Poems*, *The Day Before: New Poems*, and *Ode to the Cold War: Poems New and Selected*, all published by Sarabande Books. He has received NEA and Ingram Merrill Fellowships in Poetry Writing, as well as a Pushcart Prize and numerous other national honors. Other of his new poems recently have appeared in or are forthcoming in *American Poetry Review*, *Buddhist Poetry Review*, *Plume*, *Baltimore Review*, *Tricycle*, *Able Muse*, *Café Review*, and *The Hudson Review*.

MAUREEN ALSOP, is the author of *Mantic*, *Apparition Wren*, *Later, Knives & Trees*, and *Mirror Inside Coffin* (forthcoming). Her poems have appeared in numerous magazines including *Kenyon Review*, *Tampa Review*, *Typo*, and *Barrow Street*. She edits poetry for *Poemeleon*, and teaches locally through the Inlandia Institute and online with the Rooster Moans poetry cooperative. Her website is www.maureenalsop.com.

RAE ARMANTROUT's most recent book, *Just Saying*, was published by Wesleyan in 2013. A new book, *Itself*, is forthcoming in 2015. Armantrout's volume *Versed* (Wesleyan) won the 2010 Pulitzer Prize in Poetry as well as the National Book Critics Circle Award. She lives and teaches in San Diego.

DAVID B. AXELROD, is celebrating the publication of his 21st book, *Rusting: Ways to Keep Living*. A three-time Fulbright Award winner, he served Suffolk County, Long Island, as Poet Laureate from 2007-2009 and is now director of the Creative Happiness Institute in Daytona Beach, Florida. His websites are: www.poetrydoctor.org and www.creativehappiness.org.

WALTER BARGEN has published eighteen books of poetry. His most recent books are *Days Like This Are Necessary: New & Selected Poems* (2009), *Endearing Ruins/Liebenswerte Ruinen* (2012), *Trouble Behind Glass Doors* (2013), *Quixotic* (2014), and *Gone West* (2014). He was appointed the first poet laureate of Missouri (2008-2009). His website is www.walterbargen.com.

FRED BASSETT is a Biblical scholar, novelist, and award-winning poet whose poems have been widely published in journals and anthologies. He has two books of "found poetry" that he created from the lyrics of the Bible: *Love—The Song of Songs* and *Awake My Heart: Psalms for Life*. *The Old Stoic Faces the Mirror* is his latest collection of poems. In addition, he has two published novels of a planned trilogy, *South Wind Rising* and *Honey from a Lion*. Now retired from academia, he lives with his wife Peg near their grandchildren in Greenwood, South Carolina.

JACK B. BEDELL is Professor of English and Coordinator of Creative Writing at Southeastern Louisiana University where he also edits *Louisiana Literature*, a nationally-recognized literary journal, and directs the Louisiana Literature Press. His latest collections are *Bone-Hollow, True: New & Selected Poems, Call & Response, Come Rain, Come Shine, What Passes for Love*, and *At the Bonehouse*, all published by Texas Review Press (a member of the Texas A&M Press Consortium). Dr. Bedell recent work appears in the *Southern Review, Hudson Review, Connecticut Review, Paterson Literary Review, Texas Review, Southern Quarterly*, and other journals. He and his wife Beth have three children, Jack, Jr., Samuel Eli, and Emma Louise.

CHARLES BERNSTEIN, author of *Recalculating* (University of Chicago Press, 2013), *Attack of the Difficult Poems: Essays and Inventions* (University of Chicago, 2011), and *All the Whiskey in Heaven: Selected Poems* (Farrar, Straus and Giroux, 2010), currently teaches at the University of Pennsylvania. To learn more, visit epc.buffalo.edu.

JOYCE BRINKMAN, Indiana Poet Laureate (2002-2008), believes in poetry as public art. She creates public poetry projects involving her poetry and the poetry of others. Her own poetry is on permanent display in a twenty-five foot stained glass window at the Indianapolis International Airport, in lighted glass artwork at the Central Indianapolis Public Library, and on a wall in the town square of Quezaltepeque, El Salvador. She is a founding board member of the nonprofit organization, Brick Street Poetry Inc. Joyce has received fellowships from the Mary Anderson Center for the Arts, the Indiana Arts Commission, and the Arts Council of Indianapolis. *Seasons of Sharing: A Kasen Renku Collaboration*, which she wrote with Carolyn Kreiter-Foronda and four international poets, will be out in September of 2014. She is a graduate of Hanover College and lives in Indianapolis, Indiana with her husband and a sweet cat.

JOHN J. BRUGALETTA taught Shakespeare, Dante, and Homer for thirty years at Cal State Fullerton. He edited and published *South Coast Poetry Journal* for ten years, then saw two of his poetry books, *The Tongue Angles* and *With My Head Rising Out of the Water*, both published by Negative Capability Press. Dr. Brugaletta has had four other books, 17 articles, and about 170 poems in 57 periodicals. After retiring, he and his wife moved to the far northern end of California, where he builds structures to save a few of their roses and fuchsias from the deer. Once in a while he writes a poem.

JOE CAVANAUGH was born in Providence, Rhode Island in 1941. He earned a B.A. from Georgetown University (1963) and an M.A. from SUNY Buffalo (1967.) His three published collections of poetry, *Poetry Jam with Toast and Tea* (Writers Ink Press, 2010), *California Dreamin*, (Creative Happiness Institute, 2012) and *Love Happens* (Create Space, 2014) are available from Amazon.com or directly from the author. He likes to tell stories, perform, share poetry and hang out with poets and poetry lovers. He is currently the President of the Florida State Poets Association.

J. WILLIAM CHAMBERS lives in Athens, Alabama. He is author of *Camellias in Autumn* (Honeysuckle Imprint, 1989), *A Taste of Wine and Gentian* (Negative Capability Press, 2000), and *Suite for Stefano and Luisa-Gatta* (Negative Capability Press, 2012). He is editor of and contributor to *Collage: A Tribute to Steven Owen Bailey* (Negative Capability Press, 2006) and co-editor and contributor to *Whatever Remembers Us: An Anthology of Alabama Poetry* (Negative Capability Press, 2007). In 2009 he published *Steve's Story: A Memoir* (Elk River Review Press, 2009). His poetry, reviews, and essays have been widely published in numerous journals and magazines. He was founding editor and publisher of *Elk River Review* (1990-1999). In 1987 he was awarded the Distinguished Alumnus Award from Athens State University, and in 2011 he was awarded the Alabama State Poetry Society's Poet of the Year.

KELLY CHERRY is the author of 22 full-length books, nine chapbooks, and two translations of classical drama. Her most recent title is *A Kind of Dream*, a collection of linked stories, selected by Library Journal as a Best Indie book. Her most recent book of poems is *The Life and Death of Poetry* (LSU, 2013). *A Kelly Cherry Reader* is forthcoming in fall 2014.

PETER J. COOLEY has published nine books of poetry, eight of which were published by Carnegie Mellon including his latest release, *Night Bus to the Afterlife* (2014). He is currently Senior Mellon Professor of English and Director of Creative Writing at Tulane University in New Orleans, Louisiana.

CHRIS CRITTENDEN has published over six hundred poems in numerous journals, many of which have strong academic or colloquial reputations including *Chelsea, Atlanta Review, Portland Review, Disquieting Muses Quarterly, Blue Unicorn, Barnwood, The 2River View*, and *Harpur Palate*. His ninth chapbook, *Rebellion*, recently won first place in *The Medulla Review* competition. He has been interviewed on KPFK's *Poets Café* and *Jane Crown's Poetry Radio*. Many influences impact his daily passion for writing, some of which are: a Ph.D. in philosophy which grounds his ecofeminist ethos; a life spent almost equally on the east and west coasts (he now resides in a tiny fishing village without traffic lights); an anguished shamanic spirituality; a powerful awe and love for the miracle of life; and his marriage to a beautiful, artistic, supportive woman whose sculptures, paintings, and tapestries surround and amaze him.

EMMANUEL DAMON lives in Paris and in the Val-de-Loire, France. He has published several books of poetry. His latest, *Archipel du soleil liquide*, with paintings by his father, the painter Hubert Damon, was published by Al Manar in 2013.

KRISTINA MARIE DARLING is the author of seventeen books, which include *Melancholia (An Essay)* (Ravenna Press, 2012), *Petrarchan* (BlazeVOX Books, 2013), and a forthcoming hybrid genre collection called *Fortress* (Sundress Publications, 2014). Her awards include fellowships from Yaddo, the Helene Wurlitzer Foundation, and the Hawthornden Castle International Retreat for Writers, as well as grants from the Kittredge Fund and the Elizabeth George Foundation. She is currently working toward a Ph.D. in Poetics at SUNY Buffalo State in Buffalo, New York.

JOHN DAVIS JR. holds a MFA from University of Tampa and his poetry has been nominated for the Pushcart Prize. His book, *Middle Class American Proverb*, is published by Negative Capability Press.

NANDINI DHAR is the author of the chapbook *Lullabies Are Barbed Wire Nations* (Two of Cups Press, 2015). Her poems have recently appeared or forthcoming in *Word Riot, Potomac Review, PANK, Los Angeles Review,* and elsewhere. She is the co-editor of the journal *Elsewhere*. She hails from Kolkata, India, and divides her time between her hometown and Miami, Florida, where she is an Assistant Professor of English at Florida International University.

MELISSA DICKSON's collections include *Cameo* (2011) and *Sweet Aegis, Medusa Poems* (2013). Her poems can be found in *Shenandoah, North American Review, Bitter Southerner, Southern Humanities Review, Cumberland River Review, Southern Women's Review, Literary Mama,* and *Gravy* from the Southern Foodways Alliance at the University of Mississippi. She holds an MFA in Visual Arts from the School of Visual Arts, an MFA in poetry from Converse College, and a BFA from Auburn University.

CHANTAL ENRIGHT, born in Paris, has spent lengthy periods in Mexico and Spain. Since 1987, she divides her life between Argentina and France. She has participated in numerous literary workshops in both countries. She has published several collections of poems. In Argentina: *Rizoma en Nocturno Vuelo,*

Nino Huerfano, and *Sangre del Tiempo*. In France, she has published bilingually in *Les Cahiers Bleus*, and edited and translated a collective work: *Voix of Argentine*. Chantal is married to the Argentine painter Ronaldo Enright.

BETH ANN FENNELLY directs the MFA Program at the University of Mississippi, where she was named Outstanding Teacher of the Year. She's won grants from the NEA, the MS Arts Commission, and United States Artists. Her work has won a Pushcart Prize and three times been included in *The Best American Poetry Series*. Fennelly writes essays on travel, culture, and design for *Country Living, Southern Living, AFAR, Garden and Gun, The Oxford American*, and others. Fennelly has published three full-length poetry books (*Open House, Tender Hooks*, and *Unmentionables*) and a book of nonfiction (*Great with Child*) all with W. W. Norton. *The Tilted World*, the novel she co-authored with her husband, Tom Franklin, was published in 2013 (HarperCollins). They live in Oxford with their three children.

JENNIFER GRANT is a recovering journalist. She spent 15 years as a stressed-out writer/editor of other people's stories (from the Big Easy to the Florida Everglades) but now creates her own curiosities. Her prose poetry and flash fiction have appeared in publications such as *Apollo's Lyre, Bacopa Literary Review, Flashquake*, and *Mixitini Matrix*. She lives in Gainesville, Florida.

ROBERT GRAY is the author of three books of poems, including *DREW: Poems from Blue Water* and *I Wish That I Were Langston Hughes*, and has been nominated for a Pushcart Prize. He has also recently directed a documentary film project on race relations entitled *Mobile in Black and White*. He has taught at several universities and is currently at the University of South Alabama. He lives in Mobile, Alabama with his wife, Kim, and two children, Liam and Emma.

CAROLYN HAINES is the author of over 67 published books in a number of genres from general fiction to non-fiction and crime novels and mysteries. Her latest book is *Booty Bones*, the 14th in the popular series *Sarah Booth Delaney Mysteries*. She also writes as R.B. Chesterton. *The Seeker* is her latest gothic chiller under that pseudonym. In 2010 she was awarded the Harper Lee Award for Distinguished Writing and, in 2009, the Richard Wright Award for Literary Excellence. She is founder of Good Fortune Farm Refuge and works to rescue animals and promote animal rights and the need for spay/neuter laws in the Southern states. Her website is www.carolynhaines.com.

BARBARA HAMBY is the author of five books of poems, most recently *On the Street of Divine Love: New and Selected Poems* (2014) published by the University of Pittsburg Press, which also published *Babel* (2004) and *All-Night Lingo Tango* (2009). She was a 2010 Guggenheim Fellow in Poetry and her book of short stories, *Lester Higata's 20th Century*, won the 2010 Iowa Short Fiction Award. She teaches at Florida State University where she is Distinguished University Scholar.

GEORGE HELD, a six-time Pushcart Prize nominee, contributes poems, stories, and book reviews to such periodicals as *Commonweal, Confrontation*, and *Notre Dame Review*. He has poems in the recent anthologies *Rabbit Ears: Poems on Television* and *Obsession: Sestinas in the Twenty-first Century*. His eighteenth collection is *Culling: New & Selected Nature Poems* (2014).

BARBARA HENNING is the author of three novels and nine books of poetry. Her most recent books are a collection of poetry and prose, *A Swift Passage* (Quale Press 2013) and *Cities and Memory* (Chax Press, 2010). Born in Detroit, she has lived in New York City since 1983. She teaches for Naropa University and Long Island University in Brooklyn, where she is Professor Emerita.

ROALD HOFFMAN was born in 1937 in Złoczów, Poland. Having survived the war, he came to the U. S. in 1949 and studied chemistry at Columbia and Harvard Universities, completing his Ph.D. in 1962. Since 1965, he has been at Cornell University, currently serving as the Frank H. T. Rhodes Professor of Humane Letters, Emeritus. As a writer, Hoffmann has carved out a land between science, poetry, and philosophy through many essays, four nonfiction books, five volumes of poems, and three plays, widely produced.

RANDALL HORTON is the recipient of the Gwendolyn Brooks Poetry Award, the Bea Gonzalez Poetry Award, and, most recently, a National Endowment of the Arts Fellowship in Literature. Randall is a Cave Canem Fellow, a member of the Affrilachian Poets, and a member of The Symphony: The House that Etheridge Built. Randall is Assistant Professor of English at the University of New Haven. An excerpt from his memoir titled *Roxbury* is published by Kattywompus Press. Triquarterly/Northwestern University Press in the publisher of his latest poetry collection *Pitch Dark Anarchy*.

RAMONA L. HYMAN, is an Associate Professor of English at Oakwood University, a poet, essayist, blogger, and performance artist. She is also the founder of the African American Healers' Conference.

JULIE KANE's poetry collections include *Rhythm & Booze* (2003), Maxine Kumin's choice for the National Poetry Series; *Jazz Funeral* (2009), the winner of the Donald Justice Poetry Prize; and *Paper Bullets* (2014), a new collection of light verse. The 2011-2013 Louisiana Poet Laureate, she teaches at Northwestern State University in Natchitoches, Louisiana.

X. J. KENNEDY will have two new books published this fall: a comic novel, *A Hoarse Half-human Cheer*, and *Fits of Concision: Collected Poems of Six or Fewer Lines*.

LISSA KIERNAN is the author of *Two Faint Lines in the Violet*, and *Glass Needles & Goose Quills: Elementary Lessons in Atomic Properties, Nuclear Families*, and *Radical Poetics*. She founded and directs The Rooster Moans Poetry Cooperative, a provider of online poetry workshops.

AMY KING teaches Creative Writing at SUNY Nassau Community College and works with VIDA: Women in Literary Arts. Of *I Want to Make You Safe* (Litmus Press), John Ashbery describes Amy King's poems as bringing "abstractions to brilliant, jagged life, emerging into rather than out of the busyness of living." *Safe* was one of Boston Globe's Best Poetry Books of 2011. Check her latest blog entries at *Boston Review*, *Poetry Magazine* and the *Rumpus*.

DAVID KIRBY's collection *The House on Boulevard St.: New and Selected Poems* was a finalist for the National Book Award in 2007. Dr. Kirby is the author of *Little Richard: The Birth of Rock 'n' Roll*, which the *Times Literary Supplement* of London called "a hymn of praise to the emancipatory power of nonsense." His most recent poetry collection is *A Wilderness of Monkeys*. His website is www.davidkirby.com.

PHILIP C. KOLIN is the editor of the *Southern Quarterly* and the University Distinguished Professor in the College of Arts and Letters at the University of Southern Mississippi. Dr. Kolin has published more than 40 books on Tennessee Williams, Shakespeare, Edward Albee, and contemporary African American playwrights, especially Adrienne Kennedy and Suzan-Lori Parks. A poet as well, he has written six poetry collections, the most recent being *Reading God's Handwriting* (Kaufmann, 2012) and *In the Custody of Words* (Franciscan UP, 2013). *His Departures: A Collection of Poems* is published by Negative Capability Press.

CAROLYN KREITER-FORONDA served as Virginia's Poet Laureate from 2006-2008. She has published six poetry books and co-edited two anthologies. *Seasons of Sharing: A Kasen Renku Collaboration* is forthcoming in fall of 2014. Her poems have received numerous awards and appear widely in journals, including *Nimrod*, *Prairie Schooner*, *Mid-American Review*, *Best of Literary Journals*, and *Poet Lore*. An accomplished painter and educator, she teaches art-inspired writing workshops for the Virginia Museum of Fine Arts.

HANK LAZER has published seventeen books of poetry, including *Portions* (Lavender Ink, 2009), *The New Spirit* (Singing Horse, 2005), *Elegies & Vacations* (Salt, 2004), and *Days* (Lavender Ink, 2002). In 2008, *Lyric & Spirit: Selected Essays, 1996-2008* was published by Omnidawn. His seventeenth book of poetry *N18 (complete)*, a handwritten book, is available from Singing Horse Press: www.singinghorsepress.com/titles/n18/Pages from the notebooks have been performed with soprano saxophonist Andrew Raffo Dewar at the University of Georgia and in Havana, Cuba. Recent features on the Notebooks appear in *Talisman #42* (including an interview conducted by Marjorie Perloff) and *Plume #34* (including a conversation with Glenn Mott, and an mp3 of a performance with Andrew Raffo Dewar). Audio and video recordings of Lazer's poetry and an interview for Art International Radio can be found at Lazer's PennSound website: www.writing.upenn.edu/pennsound/x/Lazer. html.

DENISE LOW, second Kansas Poet Laureate, has published 25 books, including *Mélange Block* (Red Mountain Press) and *Ghost Stories* (*The Circle*—Best Native American Books of 2010; Ks. Notable Book). Low's *Natural Theologies: Essays* (The Backwaters Press, 2012) is the first critical review of mid-plains literature. Low is a former board member and past president of AWP. She writes articles, blogs, and reviews and also publishes a small press, Mammoth. More information about Low can be found at http://deniselow.blogspot.com or www.deniselow.net .

JOHN C. MANNONE has work in *Split Rock Review*, *Agave*, *BlazeVOX*, *Tupelo Press*, *Raven Chronicles*, *Poetica Magazine*, *Synaesthesia*, *3Elements Review*, *The Baltimore Review*, *Rose Red Review*, *Pirene's Fountain*, *Tipton Poetry Journal*, *Prairie Wolf Press Review*, *The Pedestal* and others. His collection, *Flux Lines*, was a semi-finalist for the 2013 Mary Ballard Poetry Chapbook Prize. He's the poetry editor for *Silver Blade* and *Abyss & Apex*, and an adjunct professor of physics in east TN. His work has been nominated three times for the Pushcart. Visit *The Art of Poetry*: http://jcmannone.wordpress.com.

DAMON FERRELL MARBUT is author of the critically-acclaimed novel *Awake in the Mad World* (2012) and the Amazon bestselling poetry collection *Little Human Accidents* (BareBackPress, 2012). Originally from Mobile, Alabama, he now lives and works in New Orleans.

IRENE MARKS, translator and Professor of Spanish Language, Literature and Latin, was born in Buenos Aires and currently works as a teacher and translator.

MICHAEL MARTONE was born in Fort Wayne, Indiana. He has taught at several universities including Johns Hopkins, Iowa State, Harvard, Alabama, and Syracuse. He participated in the last major memo war fought with actual paper memoranda before the advent of electronic email. Staples were deployed. The paper generated in that war stacks several inches deep, thick enough to stop a bullet. Martone learned that the "cc:" is the most strategic field of the memo's template, and he is sad to realize that fewer and fewer readers know what the "cc:" stands for let alone have ever held a piece of the delicate and duplicating artifact in their ink stained and smudged fingers. It, like everything else, is history.

CARLO MATOS has published four books of poetry. His latest book, *The Secret Correspondence of Loon and Fiasco*, is forthcoming from Mayapple Press later this year. His poems, stories, and essays have appeared in such journals as *PANK*, *Paper Darts*, *The Rumpus*, and *HTML Giant*, among many others. He lives in Chicago, Illinois where he teaches writing at the City Colleges of Chicago by day and trains kickboxers and cage fighters by night. After hours, he can be found entertaining clients at the Chicago Poetry Bordello.

PETER MEINKE has been Poet Laureate of St. Petersburg, Florida since 2009. He has published over 20 books. *Lucky Bones*, his eighth collection in the prestigious Pitt Poetry Series, will be published early in 2014. In recent years, in addition to this year's book, the University of Tampa Press has published *Lines from Neuchâtel* (2009) and *The Shape of Poetry: A Practical Guide to Writing & Reading Poems* (2012), all illustrated by his wife Jeanne. His work has appeared in *The New Republic*, *The New Yorker*, *The Atlantic*, *Poetry*, and dozens of other journals. His collection of stories, *The Piano Tuner*, won the 1986 Flannery O'Connor Award. Peter has received two National Endowment of the Arts Fellowships, and three awards from the Poetry Society of America, as well as various PEN and O'Henry Awards for his short stories. He retired from Eckerd in 1993 and has been writer-in-residence at many colleges and universities.

TEAL MIMS is the Vice President of the Florida State Poetry Association. He is a graphic artist and President of Mims Surveying & Mapping in the State of Florida and an award-winning poet. He was employed by the prime contractor on the Apollo Moon mission in the 1960s.

CARYN MIRRIAM-GOLDBERG, Ph.D., is the 2009-2013 Kansas Poet Laureate, author of 19 books (including poetry, a bioregional memoir, novel, and book about the Holocaust), and coordinator of Transformative Language Arts at Goddard College. Her most recent books are *Chasing Weather*, a collaboration of Caryn's poetry and Stephen Locke's storm chasing photography (Ice Cube Press), and *Poem on the Range*, a memoir about her poet laureate years (Coal City Press). A beloved writing workshop facilitator, she is certified in poetry therapy, yoga and Curvy Yoga, group facilitation, and grassroots organizing. Her website is www.carynmirriamgoldberg.com.

ROBERT MORGAN is the author of fourteen books of poetry, most recently *Terroir*, 2011. He has also published nine volumes of fiction, including *Gap Creek*, a New York Times bestseller. A sequel to *Gap Creek*, *The Road From Gap Creek*, was published in 2013. A new novel, *North Star*, is forthcoming in 2015. In addition he is the author of three nonfiction books: *Good Measure: Essays, Interviews, and Notes on Poetry*; *Boone: A Biography*; and *Lions of the West: Heroes and Villains of the Westward Expansion*, 2011. He has been awarded the James G. Hanes Poetry Prize by the Fellowship of Southern Writers, and the Academy Award in Literature by the American Academy of Arts and Letters. In 2013 he received the History Award Medal from the DAR. Recipient of fellowships from the Guggenheim and Rockefeller foundations, the National Endowment for the Arts, and the New York State Arts Council, he has served as visiting writer at Davidson College, Furman, Duke, Appalachian State, and East Carolina universities. A member of the Fellowship of Southern Writers, he was inducted into the North Carolina Literary Hall of Fame in 2010. Born in Hendersonville, North Carolina, October 3, 1944, he has taught since 1971 at Cornell University, where he is Kappa Alpha Professor of English.

MARY MURPHY has presented her poetry at the Library of Congress in Washington D.C. and the Alabama Book Festival in Montgomery, Alabama. A diverse writer, and health care worker for years, she has also written several magazine articles dealing with various health issues. Murphy's book of poetry *Blama: Sound of the Wounded Word* was published in 2013 and she is now completing her next collection. She works as an English instructor at the University of South Alabama.

JANET PASSEHL is an internationally exhibited visual artist as well as a poet, and she has participated in several cross-genre projects based in the UK. She received an MFA in creative writing/poetry from Stonecoast Writers' Program in 2010. Her poems have been published in *Court Green, Arsenic Lobster,* and several issues of *Caliban Online*. An image of her 2011 installation "Dam" is forthcoming in *Ploughshares*. Janet lives in Essex, Connecticut, with her husband Chris, their greyhound Lee Lee Belle, and the ghosts of greyhounds past.

P.T. PAUL was chosen as 2014 Poet of the Year by the Alabama State Poetry Society and is the featured poet on "Culturally Speaking with Tod Jonson, Man About Town" on WABF-AM 1220 Fairhope. She received her BA in English from the University of Montevallo, and her MA in Creative Writing from the University of South Alabama. Her thesis, *Southerner*, was published as *To Live & Write in Dixie* by Negative Capability Press. She is president of the Pensters Writing Group and Vice President of the Alabama Writers Conclave. Her poetry has been published in the 10th anniversary edition of *Literary Mobile, Oxford American Magazine, Birmingham Arts Journal, Avocet - A Journal of Nature Poems*, the Austin International Poetry Festival's anthology, the Limestone Dust Poetry Festival's anthology, *Tower, Oracle Fine Arts Review*, and other publications. She lives on the Eastern Shore of Mobile Bay with her husband Larry Sampson.

MAJORIE PERLOFF teaches courses and writes on twentieth and now twenty-first century poetry and poetics, both Anglo-American and from a Comparatist perspective, as well as on intermedia and the visual arts. Dr. Perloff is Professor Emerita of English at Stanford University and Florence R. Scott Professor of English Emerita at the University of Southern California. She is an elected fellow of the American Academy of Arts and Sciences and the American Philosophical Society. Her most recent book is *Unoriginal Genius: Poetry By Other Means In The New* (Chicago, 2010; paperback 2012). Her memoir *The Vienna Paradox* (2004) has just been translated into German and Portuguese. A collection of interviews and essays will be published in fall 2014 by The University of Chicago Press under the title *Poetics In A New Key*.

MARGE PIERCY's 18th poetry book, *The Hunger Moon: New & Selected Poems, 1980-2010*, was published in paperback by Knopf in 2011. Others poetry collections include *The Crooked Inheritance, Colors Passing Through Us, What Are Big Girls Made Of,* and *The Art Of Blessing The Day*, which are all now in paperback, in addition to the earlier selected poems *Circles On The Water*. Piercy has also published 17 novels including *Gone To Soldiers, Woman On The Edge Of Time, He, She And It,* and most recently *Sex Wars*. PM Press recently republished *Dance The Eagle To Sleep, Vida,* and *Braided Lives* with new introductions. Her memoir is *Sleeping With Cats* (Harper Perennial, 2002). In the spring of 2014, PM Press published her first short story collection, *The Cost Of Lunch, Etc.* Her work has been translated into 19 languages and she's given readings, workshops, and lectures at well over 450 venues here and abroad. Her website is www.margepiercy.com.

NICHOLAS RINALDI's work has received high praise in literary reviews, from the *New York Times* and the *Washington Post* to *Elle Magazine*, *The Economist*, *Publishers Weekly*, and many other venues. Three collections of his poems have appeared thus far, and three novels. A fourth novel—*The Remarkable Courtship of General Tom Thumb*—was published by Scribner August 12, 2014. He has been the recipient of numerous awards, including the Artist of the Year Award (2007), the All Nations Poetry Award, and Negative Capability's Eve of St. Agnes Award. Additional information is available in Who's Who in America, International Who's Who in Poetry, Directory of American Poets and Fiction Writers, and other prominent directories.

PAT SCHNEIDER is founder of Amherst Writers & Artists and author of five volumes of poems and two books from Oxford University Press, including *Writing Alone and With Others* and *How the Light Gets In: Writing as a Spiritual Practice.* Her website is www.patschneider.com.

VIVIAN SHIPLEY's eighth book of poetry, *All of Your Messages Have Been Erased* (SLU Press, 2010), was nominated for the Pulitzer Prize. It won the 2011 Paterson Award for Sustained Literary Achievement, the 202 Sheila Motton Prize for Poetry from New England Poetry Club, and the Connecticut Press Club Prize for Best Creative Writing. She teaches at Southern Connecticut State University as Distinguished Professor of English and serves as Editor of the Connecticut Review.

BETSY SHOLL's most recent book is *Otherwise Unseeable* (University of Wisconsin, 2014). Her awards include the AWP Prize for Poetry, the Felix Pollak Prize, a National Endowment for the Arts Fellowship, and two Maine Individual Artists Grants. She teaches in the MFA Program of Vermont College of Fine Arts, and served as Maine Poet Laureate from 2006 to 2011.

JUSTIN ST. GERMAIN is the author of *Son of a Gun*, a memoir, which won the 2013 Barnes & Noble Discover Award in Nonfiction. He lives in St. Paul, Minnesota, and teaches at Hamline University.

MARILYN L. TAYLOR, former Poet Laureate of the state of Wisconsin (2009 and 2010) and the city of Milwaukee (2004 and 2005), is the author of six collections of poetry. Dr. Taylor's work has appeared in many anthologies and journals, including *The American Scholar, Poetry, Able Muse, Poetry Daily, Measure, Iris, Mezzo Cammin*, Ted Kooser's "American Life in Poetry" column, *The New York Times*, and *Hot Sonnets*, a 2010 anthology from Entasis Press. Marilyn taught poetry and poetics for fifteen years for the English Department and the Honors College at the University of Wisconsin-Milwaukee.

STEVEN TEREF is the translator of Ana Ristovic's *Little Zebras: Selected Poems* (Zephyr Press, forthcoming in 2016) and Novica Tadic's *Assembly* (Host Publications, 2009). His poetry and translations have appeared in *Aufgabe, Conduit, The Volta,* and elsewhere. He teaches writing and literature at Columbia College Chicago.

JEANIE THOMPSON's books of poems include *How to Enter the River, Litany for a Vanishing Landscape, Witness, White for Harvest: New and Selected Poems,* and most recently *The Seasons Bear Us.* She is founding director of the Alabama Writers' Forum, a statewide service organization for literary arts, and is a member of the poetry faculty in the Spalding University brief-residency MFA Writing Program. Poems from Thompson's book-length persona poem project, "The Myth of Water: Poems From the Life of Helen Keller," have appeared recently in *KROnline, The New Sound, The Louisville Review,* and *PoemMemoirStory.*

T.K. THORNE retired as a captain of the Birmingham Police Department (the first Jewish female officer) and currently serves as executive director of a Birmingham business improvement district. Both careers provided fodder for her writing, which has been published in various venues and has garnered awards, including ForeWord Reviews Book of the Year for Historical Fiction for her debut novel, *Noah's Wife.* In 2013, the *New York Post* featured her non-fiction book, *Last Chance for Justice: How Relentless Investigators Uncovered New Evidence Convicting the Birmingham Church Bombers* on their list, "Books You Should Be Reading." A short film from her screenplay *Six Blocks Wide* was a semi-finalist at the international A Film for Peace Festival in Italy. Her next historical novel, *Angels at the Gate: the Story of Lot's Wife,* is scheduled for release fall 2014. She writes on a mountaintop, often with two dogs and a cat in her lap.

DIANE WAKOSKI's *Emerald Ice: Selected Poems 1962-1987* won the William Carlos Williams Award from the Poetry Society of America in 1989. The most recent of her more than 20 collections of poetry, *Bay of Angels,* was published in 2013 by Anhinga Press, which also published *The Diamond Dog* in 2010. Now retired, Wakoski served as Poet In Residence and University Distinguished Professor at Michigan State University from 1975 to 2012.

MARGARET WATSON is a landscape artist, designing gardens and open spaces. She is a practicing poet with a turn toward nature on the page. After attending the Landscape Program at Harvard University and the School of the Museum of Fine Arts Boston (with a Traveling Scholar Prize), she attended the American Academy in Rome and now lives in Lincolnville, Maine.

ISABELLE WHITMAN grew up in Mobile, Alabama, and Blois, France. Until recently, she ran an education and re-entry program for inmates at Orleans Parish Prison. Her work has appeared in *Whatever Remembers Us: An Anthology of Alabama Poetry* and Cambridge Press' *Media, Technology, and The Imagination*. Isabelle is completing her MA in English at the University of New Orleans, where she is editor of the Reviews section of Bayou Magazine's online blog, and is currently working on a book about her experiences in the prison.

CAREY SCOTT WILKERSON, poet and dramatist, is author of two poetry collections, *Threading Stone* and *Ars Minotaurica*. His play, *Seven Dreams of Falling*, premiered in 2013 at the historic Lillian Theatre in Los Angeles, is scheduled for two further West-Coast performances in the 2014-15 season, and is in development as an opera with composer Dale Lyles. His new play, *Two Men, Three Hats*, has been optioned by DivaWorks Productions and will premiere in Los Angeles in 2015. He holds an MFA from Queens University of Charlotte, and teaches at Columbus State University.

CHRISTIAN WIMAN is the author of numerous books. He teaches at the Yale Institute of Sacred Music. A former Guggenheim fellow, Wiman served as the editor of *Poetry* magazine from 2003 to 2013. He has taught at Stanford University, Northwestern University, Lynchburg College, and Yale Divinity School.

AMY WRIGHT is the Nonfiction Editor of Zone 3 Press and the author of four poetry chapbooks. She also received a Peter Taylor Fellowship for the Kenyon Review Writers Workshop and was recognized as an Emerging Writer in Nonfiction at the Southern Women Writers' Conference at Berry College. Her work appears or is forthcoming in a number of journals including *Bellingham Review, Brevity, DIAGRAM, Drunken Boat, Tupelo Quarterly Review, Kenyon Review, Western Humanities Review, Quarterly West, Denver Quarterly*, and *Passages North*.

SUBMISSION OPPORTUNITIES

NEGATIVE CAPABILITY POETRY BOOK CONTEST

CONTEST DETAILS: A prize of $2000, manuscript publication, and 25 copies will go to a single winner. Two runner-ups will be chosen for publication. Manuscripts that do not win will be considered for regular publication in the future. The final judge is Amy King of New York. We will promote select work of the top three winners on Twitter, Facebook, and other venues.

SUBMISSION PERIOD / DEADLINE: All entries must be submitted online between June 18, 2014 and March 13, 2015. Please do not make revisions once your work is submitted; the winner will be given an opportunity to work with an editor before the manuscript is published.

SUBMISSION GUIDELINES: All entries and payment should be made online through Submittable.
Manuscripts should be a minimum of 50 pages to a maximum of 125 pages.

ENTRY FEE: $25.00 per manuscript. Entry fees will not be refunded for manuscripts withdrawn by the author.*

§

HEALTH & WELLNESS ANTHOLOGY

We are currently accepting poetry, fiction, creative nonfiction, flash-nonfiction, flash-fiction, and hybrids for our Health & Wellness anthology.

SUBMISSION GUIDELINES: Only submit work pertaining to the theme of Health and Wellness. It can be taken literally or abstractly; have fun with it.

You may submit up to 3 poems in addition to prose works. Prose should be 10 pages or less. To be considered, work must be submitted online via our Submittable page. The deadline to submit is April 6, 2015.

Detailed submission guidelines for all opportunities can be found at
www.negativecapabilitypress.org/contests

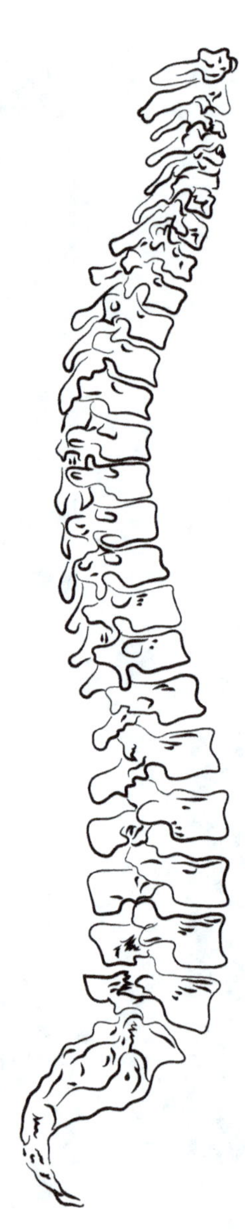